D1590648

6-26

THE TARES AND THE GOOD GRAIN

---

or the Kingdom of Man at the Hour of Reckoning

THE TARES AND THE GOOD GRAIN

or the Kingdom of Man at the Hour of Reckoning

by

Tage Lindbom

Translated by

Alvin Moore, Jr.

ISBN 0-86554-079-9

Originally published in Swedish
under the title *Agnarna och Vetet*, translated
into French by Roger Du Pasquier of Switzerland
and published by Archè, Milan,
under the title *L'Ivraie et le bon grain,*
ou le royaume de l'homme à l'heure des échéances, this
translation from the French is by Alvin Moore, Jr.

All books published by Mercer University Press are produced
on acid-free paper that exceeds the minimum standards set by the
National Historical Publications and Records Commission.

Library of Congress Cataloging in Publication Data

Lindbom, Tage, 1909-

The tares and the good grain, or, The kingdom of man at the hour of reckoning.

Translation of: Agnarna och vetet.

Bibliography: p. 141

1. Civilization , Modern. 2. Secularism.
3. Regression (Civilization) 4. Man (Christian theology)
5. Religion—Philosophy. I. Title. II. Title: Kingdom of man at the hour of reckoning.

CB358.L5613 1983 909 83-944
ISBN 0-86554-079-9

TABLE OF CONTENTS

TRANSLATOR'S PREFACE

The book here offered, *The Tares and the Good Grain*, by Tage Lindbom, is not an exegesis of the Gospel parable which is known by that name—at least, not directly—notwithstanding the title. It is rather an exposition of evidence from the fields of individual and social psychology, political science, history, and concordant traditional doctrine regarding man's life in society and the life of society itself. It is a sketch of the bastard birth of the now almost all-pervasive Kingdom of Man, as this has come about by way of separation from and rejection of the Kingdom of God. Certainly, the tensions between a celestial and an exclusively terrestrial vocation for human beings are no recent discovery. The ancient Greeks knew of an innate urge, the gift of Heaven, that impels some men towards the celestial pilgrimage; and of other impulsions that draw men downwards. We have Plato's doctrine of an inner Acropolis and an outer mob, whether in the State or in the individual; and the dichotomy appears again and again, explicitly or implicitly, in the Gospels. St Augustine long meditated upon and wrote extensively about these themes while Rome was in the later stages of decline, and he lived out his last days while the Vandals were besieging his cathedral city of Hippo.

In our own time we, too, are under siege by vandals yet more wantonly destructive and contemptuous of every civilized value than those Augustine knew. Our own cosmic "moment" is similarly situated amidst another decaying civilization, but with dangers more pervasive, more subtle, more irrevocable. Dr. Lindbom identifies many of these threats to orderly life, especially those that are manifested socially in our own times and in the intellectual life of the last several centuries in the modern West. He relates these to principles, thus making clearer their probable development and that of the Kingdom of Man. He brings to this task great erudition and great intellectual penetration into sociological matters, plus acute insights into the motivations of modern social movements. This is one of the remarkable values of the book—that the qualitative nature of our times is rendered so much clearer through social evidence, reaching us thus on terrain with which we are already generally familiar. We believe that the book will be of great interest to those of conservative persuasions, Americans especially, and English language readers generally. "Conservative" is an honorable appellation, meaning as it does defender or protector; but—let it be frankly stated—so often those who bear that name need not a little *approfondissement* of their views. This book can be of much help in a furtherance and deepening of our understanding of the decline of our institutions and the decay of civilized life, phenomena which we see all around us. The book will also be of great interest to the authentic "moral majority," all those who "love justice and hate iniquity" and who desire that justice prevail in their personal lives and in the life of the nation.

It must be pointed out, however, especially to these latter, that the author frequently has recourse to doctrine drawn from outside the Christian tradition, that is, from other religions—but always from orthodox readings. Recognizably, this may be offensive to some devout Christian readers whose sound instincts are to remain strictly within the confines of their own traditional form. In these times of our own great indigence, however, one must try to discern truth wherever it may be encountered. In the words of St. Ambrose, "all truth, by whomsoever spoken, is from the Holy Spirit," which would indeed be obvious if we had a more adequate doctrine of the Spirit, or rather of the Spirit/Intellect. It is a certainty that *Spiritus ubi vult spirat*, "the Spirit bloweth where it listeth," and that it is not bound by our conventional views. In these last times when we are truly *in extremis* intellectually and socially, we need help from wherever it may be available; for, unfortunately, the institutions of our own Christianity are decrepit and, not infrequently, in an even worse condition. Let us admit our need, then, and gratefully accept intellectual succor from our spiritual neighbors. We may in this way, *Deo volente*, come to a better understanding of our own doctrine and perhaps eventually "drink water from our own wells."

To those who might respond with questions such as these: what can an individual do in the midst of a generalized Gadarene descent such as we observe all about us? Of what use is individual effort in a world so alien not only to the life of the Spirit, but even to rudimentary virtue and the simplest responsibilities? The answer in both cases is: much more than you may think. But in any event, it is not possible to opt out of the struggle; for those who love the truth have the correlative vocation to proclaim and defend it, to push upstream, to go countercurrent; if we do not choose to exert our efforts for the good, we consent thereby to the spirit of negation and are accordingly diminished and quite possibly doomed. Man can work out his salvation in very unpromising circumstances, and it is arguable that most men do precisely this; but no one can wait for perfect or even assuredly favorable surroundings. Our efforts towards the good, the true, the beautiful are not in vain even if these efforts produce little in the way of palpable results. Human actions have cosmic ramifications, affecting in subtle and even physical ways this world which for a time we occupy, as well as affecting ourselves. Part of the equation, woven into the very web of the universe, runs something like this—*salvo meliori judicio*: every act—and in this context, thoughts, too, are "acts"—every act and every purposeful thought represents a rupture of an equilibrium of forces; and this rupture sends forth reverberations into the animate substance of the cosmos. Propagated to their maximum extent, these reverberations return inexorably as "concordant reactions" to their source, whether the actor or thinker be in this life or in some other. One reaps what one has sown. We literally shape our own destiny for our weal or for our woe, as well as affecting the world around us and even other worlds. Man can contribute, by his own justification, to a carryover from this world to another, to another cycle, another humanity, of all that can possibly serve as good seed to sprout and grow in that new creation. Nothing effectively done in the order of virtue, of drawing nearer to the Divine, can ever be lost. We have the enormous responsibility for our own fate, whether it is to be Divine or hellish; and we share in such responsibility for all other fallen creatures and for the earth itself while it forms our temporary home. "Men must bear their going hence even as their coming hither. Ripeness is all" (*King Lear*, 5.2.9).

Popularity, statistics, opinion, have no determining role in these matters. The multitudes, now as of old, are enthralled by sets of images, shadows, and illusions with which they are content and in which they do not wish to be disturbed. But when received conventions are in full dissolution, there is little reason for anyone capable of reflection to remain conventional in his inner convictions. Ripeness is indeed all, and the book here offered can be of abundant aid in our intellectual maturation.

At the end of this book, a selected bibliography will be found for the convenience of those who may wish to pursue further some of the themes adumbrated in the text.

Alvin Moore, Jr.
Carrollton, Georgia
1982

ACKNOWLEDGMENTS

Recognition and thanks are due the following: Marco Pallis, London, in the first instance, for bringing this book to my attention and urging a translation into English; Tage Lindbom, Stockholm, the author, for his generous permission, encouragement, and cooperation; Ladislao Toth of the publishing house of Archè, Milan, for his gracious permission to use the French language edition of Archè in this translation; and to Cheryl Havens, Carrollton, Georgia, for typing final copy according to the exacting requirements of computer scanning. Thanks are also due Kenneth Sapp of West Georgia College, Carrollton, for his assistance in translating several German passages; to Richard Ferrier of Thomas Aquinas College, Santa Paula, California, for identifying the elusive Greek passage in chapter 11; and last but not least my wife, Aurora, for her interest and excellent proofreading.

—Translator

INTRODUCTION

by Roger Du Pasquier

The "Swedish model" is highly prized by the non-communist world, which likes to see in it one of the finest achievements of social organization. One is disposed to believe that the Swedes have resolved the great problems of industrial society and that their example may fitly inspire other peoples, great and small, in Europe and beyond. The Swedes themselves evidently are disposed to agree, and to confer on themselves high marks of excellence; for according to a formula that resounds again and again in their discourses, *Sverige visar vager*, "Sweden shows the way." It is no doubt true that material conditions installed in what one can still call a kingdom correspond better than in any other country of the world to the ideas of social justice and even of liberty which prevail in our century, and that Sweden merits in this regard to be characterized as "model." But often less luminous aspects, sometimes very troubling aspects, have been pointed out—such problems as alcoholism, drug abuse, juvenile delinquency, or suicide have frequently commanded attention; while Sweden's reputation of extreme sexual liberty has caused not a little perplexity in foreign opinion. These phenomena are evidence that all the Swedish points of "progress" are accompanied by a moral crisis. But more often than not one regards this latter as episodic, and one persists in thinking that these problems will finally be surmounted, or that they will be controlled and "normalized," just as one often believes problems to have been resolved, even if not the least objective sign authorizes such an expectation. In any case, no one seriously doubts the ideological and philosophical bases of the system; and the conservatives, or men of the "right," when they dare show themselves, never raise any truly essential question—as witness the fact that they refer to themselves as "moderates." The Swedes therefore pursue their "debates" on the great current problems and, from their exchanges of ideas, those emerge victorious who hold that every difficulty must be resolved in a "leftward" direction, that is to say, in accentuating even more all that which seems to go in the "sense of history" and which is in conformity with the belief in the indefinite progress of humanity. Never is the opinion expressed that certain evils of society might result from an excess of modernism, of reformism, of leftism, for one wishes to search for all solutions *en avant*, the act of "looking backward" being manifestly considered a disgrace. Thus, for several years now, the question with which thinking opinion and the establishment seem most preoccupied is that of equality. True, a journal has dared publish a letter from a reader demonstrating that this is impossible to install in a living human society, and cannot be realized but in death. But no one has really paid any attention. After all, the "debate" about equality will have the effect especially of initiating a recovery of reformist zeal.

The "Lindbom phenomenon" must be situated in this context if one wishes to seize its extraordinary import. The author of the work which we here offer to the public does not represent any current of thought in his own country. He is totally isolated. But his voice, however discordant it may be in the kingdom of social democracy, is heard by those of his compatriots who even now pose to themselves questions of their final end, and who feel that the destiny of man cannot be fully accomplished at the level of social organization.

His books continue to appear with one of the most reputable publishers in Stockholm and, even if their depth and originality disconcert the critics, these qualities earn him a growing esteem in those circles capable of nonconformist reflection. For one knows that Lindbom himself possesses an exceptional fund of experience and erudition, and that, if he has turned his back on the dominant ideologies, it was truly done in full knowledge of what he was about. He had been, in fact, one of the leading thinkers of the workers' party, which he served for many years as director of their archives. And when he finally separated himself from them, he did so with no outburst. His departure was no political gesture, but response to a requirement of truth.

Born in 1909, Tage Lindbom grew up in the vast expanses of Norrland and then went to study at the University of Stockholm where he earned the degree of doctor of philosophy with a thesis on the Swedish trade union movement. From his college years he had adhered to socialist ideas and, in the course of his studies, he had even deepened his knowledge of Marxism. The social democratic party in power conferred on the brilliantly gifted young doctor the direction of its library and its central archives at its headquarters—or its citadel, if one prefers—of Norra Bantorget, in Stockholm, where, until 1965, he worked elbow to elbow with the promoters of the all-disposing State. At the beginning, he defended and illustrated with a convinced pen, the socialist ideas to which he had adhered; and certain of his works were even published in English and in German. But, man of reflection, he began to be troubled with doubts which took more precise form over the course of the years.

In Sweden, the socialist movement had undeniably gained brilliant successes. The material conditions of the working people had become very acceptable and continued to ameliorate. A good part of the claims of the workers being thus satisfied, could the movement maintain its dynamism? Could the materialist doctrines of the Marxists still provide an impetus for the working class?

In posing to himself these questions, Lindbom discovered more and more clearly this fundamental contradiction of the socialist movement which, giving priority to the satisfaction of the earthly interests of man, to his physical and vegetative demands as well as to his egotistical tendencies, at the same time appeals to his reason, to his reflective powers, to his capacity to renounce immediate advantages for more distant objectives, and even to his own disinterestedness. In order to arrive at these objectives, socialism is obliged to pose in principle that the human faculties of reason, of responsible reflection and of disinterestedness must necessarily have the upper hand over the desire to satisfy immediate sensory and passional needs.

But did the observed facts correspond to the historical evolution promised by Marxist theory, in the sense of an ever more elevated social conscience and a continuous humane and spiritual improvement? Despite the successes of social democracy, the example of Sweden amply demonstrates that all this "progress" does not lead to a future socialist citizen, creative, highly reasonable, and penetrated with a sense of civic responsibility, but rather to that of a consumer singularly desirous of rapidly satisfying the needs of his senses and easily disposed to sacrifice his socialist civic sense to his vegetative nature.

Having reached this point in his reflections, around 1950, Lindbom felt himself incapable of continuing his activity as socialist theoretician and, though remaining a party functionary, ceased to write, at least for a time. Henceforth, one question before all others preoccupied him: does man, having in his deepest nature a fundamental aspiration to perfection, have the power to respond to his aspiration by himself; can he "realize" himself by his own means, giving to his life a more lofty sense, a richer content? Gradually, a response gained ground in his mind: man cannot accomplish his superior destiny to which he fundamentally aspires without submitting himself to a superior authority, and this authority cannot be other than God.

He had to note, however, that in turning towards the churches which, normally, should have facilitated the encounter of man with God, he received from them no intellectual succor. The theological confusion to which they were prey rendered them incapable of responding consistently to the metaphysical questions of a mind such as his.

In 1959, when he had finished a work of which the very title, *The Windmills of Sancho Panza (Sancho Panzas väderkvarner)*, denounced the ideological illusions in which he had ceased to believe, his attention was drawn to a book entitled *The Forgotten Dimension (Den glömda dimensionen)*, of the Swedish writer Kurt Almquist. He finally found the opening for which he had searched, for the metaphysical knowledge which alone is capable of responding fully to the fundamental questions which confronted him. The reading of this book revealed two names: René Guénon and Frithjof Schuon, masters of traditional and universal intellectuality.

With *Man and His Becoming according to the Vedanta* and the other doctrinal works of Guénon, he became aware of the universality of truth expressed through the diverse exteriors of the sacred traditions. Schuon, in the *The Transcendent Unity of Religions*, *L'Oeil du coeur (The Eye of the Heart)*, and *Gnosis: Divine Wisdom*, notably, permitted him to discern the reality represented by the consciousness, universally diffused in humanity, of a divine Being, providence, and creator, the same for all the peoples of the earth; at the same time he understood the profound sense of the words of Christ: the Kingdom of God is within you.

Assimilating further traditional thought, thanks to other authors such as Titus Burckhardt, Ananda K. Coomaraswamy, Martin Lings, Lord Northbourne, Leo Schaya, or Seyyed Hossein Nasr, Lindbom felt himself more and more a stranger in the milieu in which he pursued his professional activity. In 1965 he drew the logical conclusion and resigned his position as head of the socialist library.

He set himself to writing and the first work witnessing to the new maturation of his thought was *Between Heaven and Earth (Mellon himmel och jord)*, published in 1970, a thorough squaring of accounts with the illusory and materialistic world of socialism. Four years later the present work appeared, of which the title, *Agnarna och vetet* (which corresponds to the biblical expression, "the tares and the good grain") suggests that the hour of great decisions formidably approaches for secularized man more and more blinded by spiritual occultation and incapable of distinguishing good from evil, truth from error. Analyzing with penetration the diverse aspects of the modernist confusion, the author vigorously denounces the progressivist illusions which poison the contemporary mentality and places us on guard against the danger we all face, that of a generalized chaos. But all hope is not lost; for the truth, transcendent and salvific, in spite of all remains accessible to men who seek it with sincerity and because the door of the divine mercy is not closed.

This work must not be regarded, therefore, simply as that of a "repentant socialist" or of a "political turncoat." Certainly the author still refers to politics and sociology of which he has such vast knowledge; but it is from a very superior point of view that he expresses himself—that of timeless wisdom found again. In the disarray in which the world is plunged today, to listen to his voice cannot but be something especially salutary.

Chapter 1
THE TIME OF HARVEST

The Declaration of the Rights of Man of 1789 is an ideological façade behind which lurk three forces: the aspiration for liberty; the desire for power; and greed. Such is the true content of the objectives of the French Revolution. The Kingdom of Man is presented as a universal proclamation: man will henceforth be a free being, all-powerful, and devoted to his own interests. He will be neither "the lord nor the slave of anyone"; he will acquire, under the form of equality, universal power; and he will "realize" himself by the satisfaction of his material needs. In principle, that implies that the human being is declared sovereign, that from henceforth he is not responsible to any superior authority and that man himself is therefore put in the place of God.

The defenders of spiritual, traditional, and conservative values who, at the time, had pronounced the condemnation of the revolution, could pass for poor prophets, for the century that followed was in many ways, for the Kingdom of Man, a triumphal march. Science and art expand. Technology continuously brings forth new tools, thanks to which men can enrich themselves through industry. Social movements lead new levels of the populace to better material conditions and to the possibility of making their influence felt on the civic level. Everything, or almost everything, bears the marks of a luminous faith in progress. "To live is a joy" proclaims the ensign of the new kingdom of happiness.

One can with reason designate the nineteenth century as the honeymoon of the Kingdom of Man. Its initial successes enhance its prestige and confidence in the future. The chaos and the bloody anarchy that the traditional and conservative forces had feared in the event of a seizure of power by the *turba incondita et confusa*, the disordered and confused multitude, did not come to pass. For the liberal community also knew how to arrange things, which it did within the cadre of the national states and of interested groups. It was not only the new forms of liberty which everywhere exercised their seduction. Everywhere man is solicited by promises of increased power in the domains of culture, of social life, and of politics. And as the masses of the people are not only concerned with liberty and power, but also with their subsistence, the new kingdom disposes new possibilities of producing new wealth thanks to technical and industrial progress.

Witnessing all this, Henri de Saint-Simon proclaims: the golden age of man is not behind, but before us. And even until our century there seemed to exist motives for having faith in progress and in a propitious development of the human community. Are the prophets of the Kingdom of Man on the right track?

The Declaration of the Rights of Man of the French Revolution is the affirmation of principles. From principle to its complete implementation, the way may be long. From one generation to the other, men live with their newly gained liberty, with their new "rights," with their new well-being. At the same time they are protected by the system of norms of the ancient order which perpetuate themselves with a surprising vigor. The defenders of the faith have not ceased to propagate their message. Popular movements of revival—principally of heterodox Calvinist origin—provided renewed nourishment to the piety of simple people. The family perpetuates itself, and with it the place of worship where the Word can be communicated to each new generation. With the family, education and modes of maturation which form new generations of responsible men, maintain themselves.

There are few things that man fears as much as chaos. This is why Western liberalism of the last century preserved so many normative elements; this is also why tradition and authority remain living realities despite all the secularization, despite all the exhortations to the contrary proceeding from the pioneers of the Kingdom of Man. The maintenance of the family and of a society wherein the sense of civic responsibility is cultivated offers an aid to a stable and normal order even in the century in which we live.

It is only since World War II that we have entered the time of the great harvest of the Kingdom of Man. We now have to deal with a secularized generation for which material existence is everything and spiritual life is nothing. It is a generation for which all that is symbolic becomes ever more incomprehensible. It is a generation which no longer lives in a viable society, but in an institutionalized world where state, administrative, and industrial apparatuses raise themselves in front of the human person like an enormous pyramid. It is a generation which is in the process of eliminating from its consciousness the notion of the family.

This generation is orphaned and this is why fraternity also loses its meaning; for, to be brothers, it is necessary to have a common father. And if there is no father, the past will appear as an absurdity. In consequence, the future will become equally absurd, for without the past there is no future. There is, therefore, nothing more than to try to lead an existence in the present, without history. One must console oneself by an "engagement" in a collective world, but without identity, and return to one's own emptiness which manifests itself exteriorly under the form of the symbiotic "community" where promiscuity must serve as a substitute for lost fraternity.

Those who have issued warnings and those who have pronounced the condemnation of the Kingdom of Man end, therefore, by being right. It is not any longer a question of predictions and warnings. We know it now, because the harvest is standing and ripe. The chaos from which we have for so long been preserved arises as a menace before us. And this menace cannot be turned aside by secular guidance except in a certain manner: by a dictatorship, a technocratic dictatorship. In reality this dictatorship has already begun to make its entrance step by step.

4 / *The Tares and the Good Grain*

The exterior chaos and this exterior menace of dictatorship are nevertheless not the essential. They are but the projection of something incomparably more serious and more dangerous—interior chaos, the confusion that reigns in the hearts of men. It is now an affair of a generation which, in its ensemble, is incapable of discerning truth from lies, the true from the false, the good from the bad. The time of harvest is come for the Kingdom of Man.

Chapter 2
PARADISE AND UTOPIA

The dramatic event which in the third chapter of Genesis is called the Fall, designates the end of the first existence of man, an innocent and paradisiacal existence. This original state of creation is characterized by an openness between the Creator and His creature; it is a state which leaves no room for opposition, neither between the work and its Author, nor within the work itself. The sun of grace and love shines on this paradisiacal state which reflects the divine light as the tranquil waters of a lake. Such is the created work at its beginning. The Lord and His work are "one" in the sense that no existential "rupture" is produced outside of the divine consubstantiality. The rapports between God and His created work know of no distance. There are heaven and earth, but the relations between them are not separative. Heaven has not let fall the curtain veiling the Author from His created work. God speaks directly to man, His image.

The biblical account of creation is one long description of a gift full of love of the Creator. It is a work which bears entirely the imprint of harmony, the absence of contradiction. It is also said that God saw all that He had created, "and it was very good." The created work in its original state is a work without fault, which has no place for evil. The whole account of creation bears the mark of this positivity. Everything receives what is its own, each living creature is assured of its subsistence and food, and first of all man, at whose disposition is found all of nature with its riches. In this existence full of serenity, where time and space are lived as a rhythmic alternation of the vegetative process itself, man lives one with nature, but equally one with God whose image he is.

Man occupies a unique position in the world, and he is invested with this position as with a mission of management; he must subdue the whole earth and reign over all the other living creatures. He is not only endowed with an immortal soul which makes him the image of God; he also possesses spiritual qualities, faculties which render him superior to every other created being, and therefore fit to carry out his mission of management.

It is there, however, that the hidden possibility of conflict lies. It is there that man meets what in biblical language is called temptation. He dominates surrounding nature in a two-fold way: he is endowed with an immortal soul, *intellectus*, which unites him to his Creator and renders him conscious of his dependence and his subordination, but he also has a reasoning capacity, *ratio*, a power which is "proper" to him, and which like his body is mortal. Why not change? Why not "liberate" himself from the ties of which his *intellectus* makes him conscious? Why not place his own mental powers in the position of greatest authority and declare himself principal possessor of power? Why not proclaim himself master of the earth?

Such is the potential threat weighing on the profound peace, the equilibrium of creation. It is not nature that poses the threat, for in its purity and innocence nature is like a mirror of the source of creation. It is man, with his wealth of faculties and his unique position, who constitutes the potential threat against the equilibrium and the peace of creation. This is why there exists one—but only one—prohibition in paradise. The prohibition is in no way directed against the creation itself. Creation, in its harmonious serenity, certainly has no need of any prohibition. It is to man that the prohibition is applied: "but you will not eat of the tree of the knowledge of good and evil, for on the day in which you eat of it, you will surely die."

It is as though the mirror of water was shattered by this prohibition. It is as if a black spot appeared on the white foundation of paradisiacal innocence. The work of creation is perfect in its cosmic harmony, in its totality. But this perfection contains also—potentially—its own negation, sin. It is this apparent paradox that confirms the omnipotence of the Creator: to the positivity of the work of creation is allied its negation, to the plus sign is allied the minus.

It is man who introduces sin into the world. He is the most elevated of all beings on earth, the image of God; but he also bears the possibilities of that which is lowest, sin and denial. This is because insofar as he is the image of God, man is a bearer of the work of creation in its totality and that is why he contains not only the highest but also the lowest, not only possibility of affirmation, but also that of negation. With man not only the divine, but also—potentially—the sinner, is found in the world. Nature does not sin, animals do not sin. It is by man that sin becomes possible in the world.

The tree of knowledge was desirable because from it one could "acquire intelligence." Through that, the way was opened for an unfolding of force. The serpent gave a glimpse of glittering possibilities; for, he said, if you eat of the fruit of the tree of knowledge, "your eyes will be opened and you will be as gods, having knowledge of good and evil." The significance of what we call the Fall is first and foremost the proclamation of human power. The earth must be subjected, man must become an independent sovereign of superior power, "to become like gods," and the path leading to this power is profane knowledge, the knowledge that man obtains by making paramount his sensory and mental faculties. Man acquires a "conscience": paradisiacal innocence disappears, man penetrates the material world and the gate of the garden of paradise closes behind him. Reason, *ratio*, is placed above intellect, *intellectus*; sensory consciousness expels suprasensible innocence: "Their eyes were opened and they knew they were naked."

This proclamation, and their exit into the sensible world, this affirmation of the primacy of rationalism, of reason—all this carried with it terrible and inevitable consequences. No one can serve two masters, and this is why the encounter with the Lord becomes a bitter recall of the veritable rapports of power and of that which man has now lost. He wishes to steal away, to hide, to disguise himself, for he no longer desires to see the face of God, to which he had so recently been accustomed. He is henceforth a "conscious" and profane being who, if he encounters the Lord, has two psychic reactions fundamentally characteristic of the profane man: fear and the feeling of culpability. He is frightened when he hears the Lord "passing through the garden" and, on encountering Him, he feels the evil of what he has done.

The first human couple certainly does not convey to us the image of those who possess power, so proud and sure of themselves, when, terrified, they endeavor to hide among the trees in the garden. But fear and the feeling of culpability are not the only effects that the fruit of the tree of knowledge procures for man. He now also knows, as the serpent promised him, what is good and what is evil. A burden that he has had to bear since then is the intimate consciousness that it is he, in going against God's command not to eat of the tree of knowledge, who has disrupted the harmony of creation. Man is a promoter of troubles. Only one prohibition had been decreed by the Master of creation, and it is this prohibition that he has transgressed. As a result of that, evil has entered into the world. The hidden conflict, which lay in the unique position of man and his potential capacity to exercise power and influence, has now become an open conflict. Man has succumbed to temptation. He wanted to be "as the gods," and by that has fallen into the fundamental sin, the greatest there is: spiritual pride, *superbia*.

The account of creation is particularly significant on this point. It shows, without ambiguity, man in possession of his free will, and fully conscious, committing an unjust action. He is thus responsible for what he has done. The first transgression of God's command committed by man, his fundamentally sinful action, is performed in the clear consciousness of desiring to obtain something in contradiction to a given order. The psychic effects also show that this act was not committed in unconscious innocence. The consciousness of the deed's evil character arouses fear on the one hand, and a feeling of culpability on the other. Moreover, that which happened is dramatic in that a separation results from it. Man no longer lives in direct communion with God, which had been the content of his paradisiacal state until now. The will of God and that of man are no longer one will. Condemnation falls rapidly and inexorably. The gate of the Garden of Eden closes.

It is not by chance that spiritual pride, *superbia*, is mentioned at the head of all other mortal sins. It is primordial in that it is a direct challenge against the divine command itself. It is an act of defiance as well as an attempt to establish a power, to institute a "world" in which man, and man alone, reigns. The other six capital sins—avarice, luxury, envy, gluttony, anger, and sloth—do not carry with them this direct attack on the divine ordinance. What the Bible describes as the Fall is dramatic not only in that from it results a separation between God and the loftiest of His created works, man; it is dramatic also in that spiritual pride, *superbia*, intervenes in a situation where a choice is offered—to obey the order of God or to follow the inclination to glorify oneself. Man chooses the latter.

It is not the "world" that is the sinner. The work of creation is, in its completeness, such as the Creator on the seventh day saw to be "very good." Good both in its organic and inorganic elements, nature appears to us with such primordiality, purity, and beauty that we are able to say that we can "see God in nature." This is why we dare say—as paradoxical as this may seem—that plants and animals possess, in their intact paradisiacal primordiality, a holiness that man does not have.

This, however, does not imply that the "world" is perfect. All created things are imperfect. To this imperfection belongs a duality that lies between, on the one hand, harmonious nature, of a vegetative character, and, on the other, a microcosmic center of energy, man, who, in his position of manager, oversteps the limits, succumbs to the temptation to disobey the most fundamental commandment of God, upsetting the cosmic equilibrium. So man introduces sin into the world.[1]

---

[1]The displacement of the center of gravity that Calvinism effects in putting emphasis on the sinful character of the world leads one to think of the terrestrial life of man as a

Secularization is a pathway leading far from the gates of paradise. Man brings with him as a traveling companion his feelings of culpability, the consciousness of what he has done. At the same time the process of secularization is a more or less conscious effort to cut all the lines of communication, to close all ways, to deny and "forget" all light that leads to the source of Truth. But secularization is more than a negative or a "forgetting"; it is also an attempt to institute an independent human existence, without superior justice, without judgment, and without mercy or pardon.

At the same time the dream of paradise remains. Amidst all the denial, the "forgetting," the secular deification of human "liberty" straining to act according to his good pleasure, even for evil, man returns continually to dreams and speculations which relate to a "deliverance" from all that is evil, discordant, and chaotic in this world which he must now conquer. He dreams ceaselessly of a state of goodness, concord, of peace and harmony.

Secular man is a "utopian" being. Though he be pessimistic or optimistic as to terrestrial existence, though he calls himself a realist or an idealist, his mind is occupied by the attempt to work out or establish an order which, he hopes, will permit him to master the oppositions of existence. Secular man lives in the multitude, the scattering, the agitation, and strife of the sensible world, and if he wishes, in such a world, to realize his proud ambitions to become an autonomous sovereign, he must be able to bring order out of chaos, unity from division. He attributes to himself the mission of abolishing the relativity of creation in claiming something which is not to be found in sensible existence itself: the absolute. And he thinks he can reach this goal by earthly means. He

---

pilgrimage through a world conceived more or less clearly as enemy territory. The "salvation" of the popular churches here takes on a dramatic character, distorting the true range of salvation while at the same time considering the completely sinful world always more and more as an object of exploitation, and this tendency is reinforced to the extent that secularization is increased. It is certainly not by chance that it was the Anglo-Saxon countries, marked by Calvinism, which were at the fore in industrial development. One must not be surprised to see a "pilgrimage" which appears to be humble and of puritan orthodoxy, become at the same time an exploitation of natural resources, an exploitation bearing the mark of spiritual pride.

believes in living in the world of reality and considers himself to be in the process of realizing his power. In fact, he loses himself in utopia.

Utopia follows secularization as shadow follows a body. It is not chance that utopia appears in the West at an epoch when the piety of the Middle Ages is definitively relegated to the background under the influence of seekers, aesthetes, and thinkers of the new age. But secularization poses new and troubling questions. Must man be abandoned to the game of natural elementary forces? Does everything finally come down to a problem of power? Will the autocrat install himself on the thrones of power and exercise an absolute and discretionary authority? Can power, conforming to Machiavelli's thesis, become an aesthetic matter, a work of art, a skillful trick, a drama without a superior norm or a ruling principle? In this case there remains little more than that which, for Machiavelli, constituted the two determining factors, *fortuna*—"destiny," and *virtù*—a concept without ethical value but rather a kind of magic elementary force thanks to which man, beyond good and evil, conquers and conserves power.

These questions have a range so much the greater as at the end of the Middle Ages, a new instrument is put at the disposition of those holding terrestrial power, the State. The young national States now have a central apparatus of power of an efficiency unknown until now. It is suggestive that utopian speculation attains its full blossoming and maturity in an epoch in which this central apparatus of power reaches its complete development in the Baroque state. The Baroque utopia is a fantastic elaboration that "resolves" the problem of power in making of life in society an architectonic and static work of art.

At the same time modern science comes to us under the appearance of utopia. The "House of Solomon," fantastic creation of Francis Bacon, is the general scientific-technical quarter wherein the savants of research and of human "wisdom," like a general staff disposing enormous powers, governs humanity, notably by manipulation, which Bacon by no means seeks to hide. The world of things must be mastered by science and cybernetics, revealing the most intimate secrets of sensible existence. Science tries to seize and enunciate in bold mathematical formulas what are taken to be the laws of nature; and, in possession of these laws, it is believed that the world of things will become the obedient servant of man.

What must be established is not only the order depending on laws and governing nature, from the march of the stars to the circulation of the blood. It is held that the life of states and society, as well as the ethical conduct of individuals, must equally be submitted to this marvelous system of laws. The eighteenth century, during which secular superstition attained its culmination—and it is that which is called the century of light!—expresses the hope that all human wisdom be brought to light, as if it could open up a golden age. It is also the century in which the classical formulations of pedagogic utopia are worked out: "natural" man, free, good, and happy, must make his appearance as the result of an education equally "natural."

With the nineteenth century there arose the familiar social movements and with them utopia entered its dynamic phase. The world must be changed, not by speculative methods, but by economic, social, and political struggles. Liberalism, socialism, communism, anarchism are the names of some of the ideologies which must show humanity the way of its anticipated liberation. Finally, we observe in the twentieth century the collapse of the scientific view of the world which we had inherited, with its faith in a system of mechanically determined laws. Even the conviction that material existence—that which secularized man calls reality—even this is revealed as false. This is what atomic physics as well as the morphological sciences have revealed. The material world is a "flux": but who will save us from perishing in this chaos of matter?

"We do not bow to the Saviour from on high," says one of the socialist songs of combat, and therefore there exists only one solution: a central government, a technocratic dictatorship. Enter cybernetics. It is a question of an implacable power exercised from central command posts and founded on statistical calculations and prognostications. This cybernetic order becomes the more necessary now that every spiritual and moral norm is on the way to dissolution—and what remains of normality when we are deprived of all norms?

Henceforth, utopia in its "classical" form no longer exists. The establishment of the universal domination of man, thanks to his rational resources and to his capacity to master the things of the world, is a dream which can persist no longer in its original forms. Man begins to doubt. He begins to doubt his own power of creation; he begins to doubt the deep meaning of historical processes. He begins to doubt whether creation may be engaged in fact in an uninterrupted progress; he begins to doubt whether secularized existence has a goal. He has thus begun to doubt even the great central utopia, the Kingdom of Man.

Does this signify the death of utopia? No, "utopianization" persists, but under new forms. Secularized man no longer "utopianizes" because he dreams of his Kingdom. He "utopianizes" because he is constrained to do so. Amidst the relativity and instability of terrestrial life, he must find points of support, "islands" from whence he may bring forth cybernetic directives. He believes that there is no other choice, for otherwise he would be engulfed in the chaos that he has himself provoked.

The color bearers of the Kingdom of Man have ended in an insoluble conflict with themselves and with their work. They had dreamed of building up a world without contradictions and they had refused to see that man is a created being, therefore incapable of "becoming like the gods." An imperfect world cannot be transformed by its own forces into a perfect work. The color bearers of the Kingdom of Man set out from the idea of a "realization of oneself" on the material level, which is a euphemism to designate human egotism. At the same time they have refused to perceive that egotism follows two guides, the desire for power and the desire for pleasure, and that these two principles, that of power and that of pleasure, are incompatible with any utopian achievement whatsoever. And even if egotism presents itself in a collective form, that of communist "fraternity," that changes nothing.

In this world marked with growing trouble, nothing is left intact. In an ever more pronounced secularization, the defenders of religion are threatened with being isolated, ignored, and misunderstood. Why not adapt oneself then, why not try to go with the current of the times, even if that must be done at the expense of truth and of justice? Adaptation, *aggiornamento*, does not date from yesterday certainly. The disposition for dialogue, for compromise, to "save what can be saved," has persisted down through the centuries. This is why the "adaptation to the conditions of contemporary civilization," in the terms of Cardinal Danielou,* is not a movement toward greater lucidity, toward an enhanced capacity to grasp divine truths, but a move towards a more dense obscurity, towards a growing confusion. If by way of dialogue, and compromise, one believes it possible to establish a *modus vivendi* between the Kingdom of God and the Kingdom of Man, one is deceived. For one cannot escape from those questions of which the compass is as independent of time and space as it is of the material and spiritual level of civilization. What is truth and what way must man follow in order to attain it? How to distinguish good from evil? How to separate the tares from the good grain?

---

*A leading French Jesuit intellectual raised to the cardinalate by Paul VI.

Chapter 3
WHAT IS TRUTH?

In the original purity of creation, man lived "beyond good and evil." Or rather he lived in a blessed detachment and in unconsciousness of [distinctions between] the true and the false, good and evil, and the just and the unjust. Today, secularized man lives extremely far from such a state. For him, on the contrary, the true, the good, and the just are constantly before him as urgent problems and burning questions. Does there exist a superior principle guaranteeing that the true does not become a lie, that the good does not become evil, that the just does not become injustice, and that human life does not turn into chaos?

Certainly one does not contest that in our secularized world there are both true and false affirmations, but what one calls true nevertheless is not recognized as something of absolute validity. The dominant conception is that truth is relative and that "each one saves himself in his own fashion," that that which is true in Halle and Jena is a bad joke in Heidelberg. For all is unstable in the Kingdom of Man. Everything is cut according to what is momentarily considered as "scientifically established," or in pursuance of what is on record as expression of the sovereign popular Will and this latter is revealed in the ballot or in public opinion polls. For the fundamental rule of the system is the unlimited sovereignty of man, and this is why no exterior power can constrain him. In short, it is what man's sensory organs give utterance to which will determine what must be regarded as true, just, and good.

The color bearers of the Kingdom of Man are nevertheless obliged to work with an *absolutum*—reality. That which, in the created material world, we experience with our senses, it is that and nothing else which is declared to be real. This reality, which secularized man conceives as absolute, is at the same time lived as a reality apprehended by our senses, limited by time and space, a reality which in all its forms of manifestation is recognized as relative. Is reality, therefore, simultaneously absolute and relative? The relativism of the truth and of the morality practiced by profane man here below, does it have a model or an absolute objective which can be attained some day? But if secularized man conceives the sensory reality in which he lives as absolute, one perceives that this is contradictory, that this reality at the same time appears as something entirely relative.

When the Creator, transcendent source of truth, is denied, nothing remains for the profane but to "seek" the truth on earth here below. And when the truth is no longer preexistent, residing in its source which is God Himself, one must conceive of it as something which may be attained somewhere out "ahead of us." The search for truth in the Kingdom of Man becomes therefore an operative process. Two ways then offer themselves to our experience, that of positivism and that of Marxism.

We find in positivism an idea inherited from the Stoicism of late Antiquity which represents truth not as an inspirated vein of gold, but as a multitude of particles of gold scattered like fragments through existence. This conception has been taken over by bourgeois liberalism and has become part and parcel of the Western notion of liberty. The fragments of truth and of falsehood are always mixed and it is a question of sorting out the noble and aureate grains of truth. Thanks to never-ending discussion, to free scientific research and to a continuous process of selection, the truth must be extricated in a progressive positivist perfectionment.

Scientific positivism finds a support even in the atomic theory of Antiquity. Epicurus maintained that the atoms, in their perpetual movement, could never encounter one another nor unite with one another to form bodies if their movement did not have a convergent tendency making them unite. The faith, so often expressed during the past two centuries, in the capacity of modern science to resolve the enigmas of existence, would be very difficult to understand from a purely psychological point of view if it did not have as underlying hypothesis notions and hopes relative to a convergence of the sensible world. This faith sometimes finds more or less explicit expressions. The physicist and Nobel prize winner, Werner Heisenberg, who surely does not limit himself to futile speculations, has expressed the hope that modern physics might be an element in the historical process leading to the unity of our world. Thus he hopes that the sciences of nature, even the cultural and other efforts of man, will finally join in a new state of equilibrium between thought and action, activity and meditation.[2]

The other way is that of Marxism. Here the truth is tied to the two Marxist pseudo-divinities, History and Matter. In the Marxist material world truth is nothing more than an ideological representation reflecting the struggles of materially determined interests. Truth, like everything else, is dominated by the historico-dialectic process and this is why the truth reigning in such and such circumstances is not other than the dominant class's conception of truth in the corresponding historic phase. The proletariat must finally emerge victor in these historic struggles and, therefore, the proletariat's conception of truth will ultimately prevail. The dialectical process, developing towards an always more elevated level, implies an end at a final state where the contradictions of existence are surmounted and where communist society without contradictions becomes the definitive state in which truth is of necessity liberated from all trace of relativism.[3]

---

[2]Jacques Chevalier, *Histoire de la pensée*, 1 (Paris, 1955), p. 461; and Werner Heisenberg, *Physics and Philosophy* (New York, 1958), pp. 205ff.

[3]For Marx there is no reality outside the world of matter or, as he also calls it, of *Praxis*; and it is in this world of matter that thought is included. Every question on the independent reality of thought is therefore senseless, as Marx states in the second of his *Theses über Feurbach*: "The question of knowing whether human thought belongs to objective truth is not a theoretical question, but a *practical* question. In Praxis, a man must prove the truth, that is to say reality and power, as being found on this side of his thought.

As a matter of fact, positivism as well as Marxism must have recourse to pseudo-metaphysical representations showing that the truth must come to meet us as scintillating and attractive gold, that the substances of truth must have a natural tendency to converge, or that the truth must "be developed" according to a historico-dialectical process in order finally to appear in its total absence of contradictions and absolute perfection. There is no reason whatsoever for us to linger over these strange speculations which are foreign to all reality. The essential is that secularized man always ardently endeavors to reach univocal representations which will deliver him from the relativism of the truth. Despite his denigration of a transcendent truth, he persists throughout generations and centuries to search painfully for assured solutions to these enigmas inherent in things.

Whence comes this effort, this indefatigable inspiration? What is it, in the final analysis, that secularized man seeks? Despite his negations, despite his avowed relativism, does he in fact search for something true which constitutes a fixed point amidst sensory existence? Truth exists for him as a concept: something exists that is true and which must be distinguished from something else that is false. Truth resides in the conscience of secularized man as a directing principle, never stifled even in the deepest darkness of secularization. Thus secularized man always wants to grasp from above the fulcrum which he constantly seeks in the concept of truth. At the same time he obstinately denies any transcendent reality, and thereby the source of truth which is in this transcendent reality. He postulates a concept of truth without knowing why, neither from whence such a concept draws its efficacy. He denies the truth even while recognizing it as a pre-existent point, and he tries to dissimulate this contradiction in holding that, thanks to profane science, the truth will finally be "discovered" as the last link in a long chain of researches.

The debate on the reality or unreality of thought—that which is isolated from Praxis—is a purely scholastic question." (Karl Marx and Frederick Engels, *Werke*, vol. 3 [Berlin, 1959], p. 5.)

That which profane man does not want to see is that the truth is found at the beginning and not at the end. That means that the truth is existentially in the created work: the truth is an expression of the positivity that characterizes all creation. This latter is thus guaranteed as order, and not insofar as blind hazard or chaos. Against this positivity the lie rises up, the "minus sign," negation. As negation of creation, the lie is perdition, ruin, annihilation—or, to return to its most profound sense—the lie is not-being, nothingness. God, manifested in His creation, *is*. "I am He who is," said Yahweh to Moses in the burning bush, and in this *is* resides truth, justice, goodness. The lie cannot be other than the negation of all this. This is why the most profound sense of untruth is not-being, nothingness.

Such is the first expression. But the truth, as expression of the positivity of creation, is only guarantor of this latter insofar as it is order—against the lie which is negation of that order. Truth is also constitutive part of the divine gift and participates as does the latter in the love which characterizes every gift and every production. Just as a child has an affinity with its parents and lives the love of this affinity, the created work is bound to its source and in the consciousness of this bond it is also lived as love. This consciousness of a bond of love with the Creator cannot rest on a negation. Thus the truth is also included in the relation of love with the Creator. Truth is in its essence united to love and this is why we do not articulate vain words where we exhort to the love of truth.

In the third place the truth is manifested in our terrestrial life. We have an awareness of something that is called truth and of something that is called untruth. Men are ceaselessly in disagreement on that which, in such and such a concrete situation, is true or false. We can have all possible controversies on the interpretation of an historical source or of statistical data. That which we concretely discuss is one thing, but the important thing is that behind these controversies is situated essentially the consciousness that truth and falsehood constitute a pair of opposites in existence.

The more accentuated secularization becomes and the more the search for truth becomes, for modern man, an affair of "things," the more he then believes that if he occupies himself sufficiently long in empirically gathering materials, classifying them, and in the structural analysis of these materials, he will arrive at something that will be indubitable and free of contradictions. For the one part he recognizes the relativity of existence; and for the other he lives in the utopian hope that, somewhere or someday, this relativity—and with it the abundance of contradictions—will be transformed into its contrary: the absolute, the univocal. That secularized man does not discover nor recognize this evident contradiction in his reflections and his aspirations is one of the most characteristic traits of the intellectual life in the Kingdom of Man.

To this is added yet another question: why does secularized man seek truth? Why this indefatigable activity? Why this feverish scientific research throughout the world? Before all else, secularized man fears chaos. Let us not forget that chaos hangs over him as a menace. The divine creation is an order, *kosmos*, and the negation of this order is, in the last resort, the contrary and satanic pole, chaos. The inhabitants of the Kingdom of Man are playing a dangerous game here; they are, so to speak, sawing off the branch on which they are perched. In their negation of the divine order and of the truth which is integrated therein, they provoke the chaos which they fear. This is why they instinctively look upwards when they lose footing, when they realize that existentially they are about to get stuck in the mud. When the prophets of secularization raise their war cries and proclaim that the reign of the "powers of darkness" must now end, that the light of truth must now spread over the earth, in reality these prophets call down the aid of the superior power which they deny.

The fear of chaos is the firm motive which pushes secularized man to try to establish a reasonable order in his existence. But how? When all values are declared relative and when everyone must "save himself as best he can," it may be tempting to make of every aspiration to the truth an affair which concerns only the egoism of the individual. But chaos is seen as a menacing possibility, and no one in modern times has described this dilemma of human existence better than Thomas Hobbs: we have to choose between a war of all against all and submission to an organized and institutionalized egoism. It is there that we are confronted with the problem of power.

The fear of chaos has a positive pole. Francis Bacon has enunciated the classical—and cynical—motivation for the profane exploration of the things of the world: knowledge is power, "human knowledge and human power meet in one."[4] Man will be the sovereign of the earth and the royal way leading to this position of power is called knowledge. But then is the search for knowledge, with the intention of obtaining a position of earthly power, the same as the search for truth? This search for knowledge envisages the acquisition of notions and aptitudes of a utilitarian and operative character. Can that be a way towards truth?

We know only too well that the response cannot be affirmative. In the world, the ambitious often manage the truth in a manner utterly devoid of scruples and, in order to come to power and to keep it, they may even be ready to annihilate the truth. The idea of power in our secularized world is in practice marked much more by cynical pragmatism than by the love of the truth. Just the opposite are those who consecrate themselves to a sincere search for truth, whom we observe as by no means animated by a desire for power.

To the desire for power and the fear of chaos, a third motive is to be added. The more our life is secularized the more it is emptied of spiritual content. When the consciousness of a transcendent reality disappears, the consciousness of creation as a totality disappears at the same time, which causes man to lose his sense of solidarity with the cosmos. The more secularization is accentuated, the more the sense of cosmic solidarity is diminished and the more man experiences existence as empty space. It is this empty space which he wants to fill with his indefatigable activity; and the more secularization progresses, the greater grows his sense of emptiness and the more man is agitated. He imagines that by his activity he

---

[4]Francis Bacon, *The New Organon, The Works*, 4, Faksimile-Neudruck (Stuttgart-Bad Cannstatt, 1962), p. 47.

can occupy this empty space, that by his organizations and his constructions of institutions he will be able to build an abode in the Kingdom of Man. In this agitation without respite, scientific activity keeps the characteristic role which has devolved upon it.

This secularized "search for the truth" involves us in an increasing pragmatism. No reasonable human being contests that scientific research has its value for our daily life. But that which is lacking in the Kingdom of Man is a corrective which responsibility before a superior power would represent. The inhabitants of the Kingdom of Man are not responsible except to one another, which is to say that the sensory needs and desires of self-interested man become, in the final analysis, the guiding thread for all life and all action. Also it is this which ultimately determines social, cultural, and scientific movements. He who wants to search for truth finds himself confronted with the growing exigency to bring together that which he estimates to be true and just with the needs and desires of self-interested man. Here the desire for power and the sensory desires of man meet in the forms of pragmatism. The principles of power and of pleasure are, in fact, found to be allies. This growing pressure of pragmatism makes one think that the ancient and more or less facetious expression according to which "the truth is unbearable," takes on an ever more bitter realism in a context of increasing secularization.

It would be quite wrong to imagine that our world could be enveloped in an impenetrable spiritual darkness. The world is not closed to the light of divine truth. In spite of all the denials, every human being remains the bearer of an intellective conscience, the "interior light" of his heart. But it would be equally false to picture to oneself divine truth as the term of a clear and evident alternative in the secularized world. We do not encounter truth and falsehood in a simple option, in the concrete and easy to make choice of an "either/or." Things are not so simple, as though a divine message might be addressed to us at the same time as the serpentine tempter might appear with a contrary message. The satanic power consists also in the capacity to disguise himself, to present himself in an attractive aspect, in such a way that the limit between the true and the false, between good and evil, might seem effaced; and even that the false can be shown in the appearance of the true, and evil under that of good. Thus it becomes possible for the subversive power to achieve his final object as formulated by Baudelaire: *La plus belle ruse du diable est de vous persuader qu'il n'existe pas.**

And finally, to search for the truth is to will the truth. Is this what I want? Such is the decisive question. But there is a prior condition: I do not love the truth if I do not will it, for, if I love the truth, I shall try to realize it also. For the truth is prior to and above the existential world and it is our duty to actualize it here below in the measure of our possibilities and to manifest it even in an existence that is imperfect and full of contradictions. Without the love of truth the will to attain it does not exist either, and without this will all choice is deprived of significance.

It is in earthly life that the problems of truth are posed to man. In original and paradisiacal existence, man was in the presence of truth as in an open and limpid relation with God. The relation was thus still that of "face to face." In our imperfect world, on the contrary, man encounters truth as a problem, and even a double problem. First, man in the world is separated from God and therefore the paradisiacal light is no longer there. This is why truth is not present to us in its crystalline obviousness. "Now we see in a mirror dimly," St. Paul said, and, in these words, he has seized the essential. The world is the inverse image, as in a mirror, of the divine truth and that is why the image does not have the vividness that the truth has in its own source. Continuous secularization makes the image in the mirror ever more diffused. The light which shines in the darkness, of which St. John speaks, in our time no longer has an obvious luminosity and its brightness is continually dimmed in progressive secularization.

Secondly, there is the fact that man, in his earthly life, constantly comes up against limits. He cannot grasp everything with his available spiritual means. If he could, he would be "as the gods," and of this he is incapable. The promise of the serpent in paradise

*"The cleverest ruse of the devil is to persuade you that he does not exist."

was false. Even our consciousness of the divine reality is a fragmentary knowledge. "My knowledge is in part," said St. Paul of that knowledge which one day must be total and plenary, when our earthly existence will be left behind.

In the first case, we experience the vertical perspective: divine truth reaches the earth like the rays of the sun which enlighten it and are reflected from it. In the second case, we are placed before the horizontal perspective: in earthly existence we come up against limits, contradictions. This is why we must, for the one part, search for truth which reaches us like the rays of the divine sun, and for the other part we must separate the truth from its existential opposite, falsehood. We do not receive the gift of truth for nothing. In order to reach the truth we have to go through a way which may be both long and painful. One must not trust all the signals and notice boards.

Chapter 4
THE WAY OF LIFE

To will is to choose, but if a choice is to have any meaning, it must be based upon an order of solid values. In the Kingdom of Man, however, all values are relative and therefore provisional. Moreover, the decisive criterion of every choice is, in final analysis, egotism, and more particularly its two determining motives, the desire for power and the satisfaction of sensory instincts. In such conditions a choice cannot truly amount to taking a position. It is nothing but a provisional act, obedient to short-sighted desires and impulses.

A choice determined in this way will not have been marked by any true grasp of responsibility, given that all are, ultimately, responsible only before themselves. The justification of their actions, finally, is only the safeguard of their own "interests" and the base of those interests is constituted only by physical needs. This is the case not only for individuals but also for collectivities, for the popular will which reigns on the collective level is in reality nothing other than a "mythologization" of accumulated human egotisms.

If I relate myself only to my desires for power and pleasure, I will never be able to grasp the truth with love. The love of the truth then becomes for me an alien concept. This is why in his aspirations to truth—which may often be worthy of interest—secularized man sooner or later ends up in pragmatism. This is also why he who has chosen the way of truth experiences his free will as a paradox: our choice is free, but we do not have the liberty to rob ourselves of choice, for if we do not say yes, we have rejected the truth. Neutralism is not possible in these matters.

Truth is one and indivisible in its transcendent source, but in terrestrial terms, the search for truth is a painful advance. For creation, like every relative thing, bears its own imperfections. This is why the truth cannot appear in its original clearness. If the way of truth was traced before us, clearly staked out so there was no possibility of our going astray, then everything created would be marked by a determination devoid of meaning: our human life would be devoid of will and of the possibility of choosing; it would be without effort and without love. Our "destiny" would be fixed in advance and creation would be a perfection, "like God." Logically, this would be an absurdity. For a work is always subordinate to its author and therefore imperfect with regard to the latter.

In relation to the Creator, creation is a reflection, an inverse image of its author. One must always remember this inversion of the reflection, source of interminable misunderstandings and false interpretations, when we try to find, from our earthly perspective, the way of truth. In the perspective of the Creator, creation follows a course from "top to bottom" but remains a cosmic unity penetrated and borne by the universal spirit. On the contrary, for us humans in our terrestrial perspective, if we cast our glance toward the nadir, we find the opposite, chaos. It is when we look towards the zenith that we perceive the cosmic totality.

We see the same thing in nature: the sea links men one to another while the mountain separates them. The transcendent aspect is the contrary: the mountain, the vertical perspective, unites with God; while the sea, horizontal perspective, binds us to the terrestrial world. In social life, material poverty is a defeat, a shirking of one's duties; and in the most difficult cases, suffering. From the spiritual point of view, poverty is just the contrary, a wealth, an affirmation, an opening to the truth. It is in this spiritual sense that the Sufi aphorism must be interpreted: "Fear the loss of poverty more than the rich fear the loss of their riches."

When we humans are searching for the truth we find ourselves with this apparently impossible task: "seize the unseizable." The essence of God—and therefore the essence of truth—is unseizable, but nevertheless we exert ourselves to affirm His reality. We "know" and "know not" simultaneously. "He who pretends to know Me, knows Me not," and inversely. We thus approach the fundamental religious problem through two dimensions: one is interior and the other exterior. God is unseizable Being, and at the same time He is apparent in the manifestation of Himself. Thus the way of truth and of life is not univocal. Our mundane condition requires us to recognize it.

Facing this duality, present from the beginning of our search for the truth, we have every reason to ask ourselves if we shall not have innumerable occasions to lose our way. Such is in fact the case. It is in following the patterns of secularization that one goes astray, for this is a flight towards the periphery, a centrifugal movement. The greater the distance of the periphery where the secularizing forces operate, and the greater the acceleration of these movements, the more rapid the variability marking all things—which offers accrued possibilities of sensory seduction. This is in fact what we observe daily in our secularized world. The more rapidly the rotation of a wheel is increased and the effect of its rotation, as it propagates the speed of the latter towards the rim, similarly the greater the acceleration of the circular movement around the sensory existentiality of the self of secularized man.[5]

The way of truth is a way towards the center, a "voyage towards the middle." Such is the interior aspect of religious reality. It is a voyage to the center as well for the spiritual as the corporeal life of man, since it is a question of the heart. Centuries of religious

---

[5]Once again we encounter here an obvious instance of the manner in which creation is an inverse image of its divine Author. Creation is transcendent in relation to a cyclic process: it has a beginning, then a cyclic path which ends when the created work returns to its Author and unites with Him. On the terrestrial level the cycle is the contrary of the above; it is a circular movement, a naturally vegetative process of life, death, rebirth, without the possibility of attaining the "center" which is the essence of the created, the Creator—not to speak of the mechanical rotation which is a flight from the center.

decadence conceding an ever greater influence to the rational and sentimental have falsified the image of the reality of religion: in the name of rationalism, the center of the true has been situated in the brain, while the heart was dethroned in order to become the abode of the sentimental. Thus man has been rendered spiritually disabled and incapable of finding the way to the sources of truth and of life.

The heart is the center of the human body, but at the same time it is the center, literally as well as figuratively, of the spiritual life. It is not a question of empty rhetoric or of pedagogical allegory when saints and sages, for thousands of years, speak of the voice of the heart, or of the eye of the heart which perceives the superterrestrial reality. This is also the reason why Jesus Christ tells us that the Kingdom of God is within us. For the heart is the abode of our immortal soul and it is this by which we participate in the divine reality. We bear this participation as a consciousness of the truth in its originality, as a function of the Divine Essence.

We have, by this spiritual consciousness which is ours, a possibility of reaching a knowledge of the truth. This knowledge is not rational; nor is it a learning acquired by our mental faculty. It is a knowledge which cannot be the object of a labor of documentation or of empirical elaboration, any more than a process of logical and discursive thought nor scientific structural analysis. This knowledge is intuitive, "direct"; it is the power of experiencing the truth which, denominated *intellectus*, must be distinguished from *ratio*, the rational faculty. This intuitive and intellective process which leads us to the knowledge of the truth and of the divine reality is not characterized by a relation of subject and object. This knowledge is a "here" and a "now" which are actualized in our spiritual consciousness. "When the light of God illumines thine understanding, cause and effect are abolished for thee," said the Persian poet Jalal-ud-Din Rumi.[6]

That does not mean that the interior and intellectual light burns ceaselessly with a clear flame and that nothing can restrain its

[6]Rumi, *Aus dem Rohrflötenbuch* (Hellerau, 1930), p. 123.

brightness. If that was the case, the children of the world would march infallibly towards a spiritual perfection under the conduct of pure thought; it is thus that Descartes imagined the development of *res cogitans*. On the contrary, the way of truth is a toilsome search up to the serenity which is reached only when man has left behind him physically and mentally the agitations and discords of life. The way of truth is not like a navigation on the agitated stream of life with various captivating decors succeeding one another without end in the scenery along the shore. The aspiration to the truth is not sustained by all the seductions and pleasurable sensations, nor by all the innumerable variety of stimulations procured by sensory existence. The way of truth and of knowledge perceived by the eye of the heart is a voyage in the opposite direction, towards serenity, towards liberty in relation to every mental "state."

As secularization proceeds, the light of truth shines with a progressively weaker brightness. But will it finally be extinguished? The champions of atheism have always acted in the conviction that the religious idea, the fruit of superstition, of ignorance, and of the propaganda of the directing and ruling classes, would disappear of itself when the light of science and of "education" could be diffused liberally over humanity. Certain appearances would seem to indicate that things really come to pass in this way. Man can be led not only to deny, but to drive away and to "forget" the intellectual consciousness. It is a question of total repudiation of conscience and of religious sensibility on the psychic level. The mental faculty then operates so powerful a "blockage" that, for it, the intuitive consciousness no longer exists.

That "victory" is precarious, however; the intellectual consciousness of a divine truth is "forgotten," driven away, blocked, but it is not dead. Atheism has given itself an objective which it cannot attain. To hunt down the immortal spirit in the world is to chase the wind. For, as Christ said in his conversation with Nicodemus, the wind blows where it will and we do not know whence it comes. For the spirit, *pneuma*—the Greek word serves also to designate the wind—it is the same. We can neither capture it, nor enclose it, nor annihilate it.

Man carries within himself the Kingdom of God; by his immortal soul, he is part of the divine. At the same time he lives in the world and is part of this world of imperfections in which he participates. This being that we are lives between "heaven and earth" and in this duality man also lives his religious life under a double rapport, interior and exterior. He possesses the Kingdom of the Heavens within himself but he has the world surrounding him and, in his sensory organs and mental faculties, he carries the world within himself. This is why man, as an earthly creature, must live his religious life on two levels.

Just as the divine truth utilizes his "language" on the interior level by the intermediary of the intuitive and intellective consciousness, God speaks to men equally on the exterior and earthly level. It is obviously not a question of language, man's specific means of communication. God does not speak in the literal sense by a sort of celestial loudspeaker. In creation, God directs us to His commandments and His word principally under two forms of manifestation, symbols and revelation.

The symbol is form. It apertains to creation and is tied therefore to forms insofar as it is a means of expression. But the symbol is not a manifestation of existential reality; it is a manifestation of that superior reality without which nothing created would be. To speak rigorously, all creation must be regarded as a single immense symbol of the creative omnipotence of God. The existential symbolizes the essential. "The world is nothing, Atma is all," says the Vedânta, and the creation or manifestation, like a mirror, reflects the brightness of the divine light. The "omnipresence" of God is an expression of double signification: on the one hand, God is everywhere present spiritually by the Spirit which penetrates all things, even inorganic matter; and on the other, He is present in a symbolic sense. This presence is therefore intellective as well as symbolic.

It is unimportant in this regard to know whether one should adopt a Ptolemaic or a Copernican world image, or whether we must see it in geocentric or heliocentric terms. The symbolic power and value of the stellar world reside in the spirituality and in the eternal truth to which they give expression, and not in rational conceptions as to its formal and material structure.[7]

The essential is that for us humans the sun rises each day as a symbol of the divine omnipotence, of rhythmic equilibrium in the created order and of the utter dependence of man in relation to the source of light and heat which is called the sun. Nature in her entirety—the rhythmic alternation of the seasons, birth, flowering, death—all is symbolic of the omnipotence of the Creator.

It is not only the great natural processes and the celestial forces which draw out life on our earth; the details of existence also witness the words of the Creator. A symbolic truth resides in the discoveries of scientific research showing that the deeper we penetrate into the world of matter, the more it becomes apparent that this matter has no "base," but that it disintegrates ceaselessly in smaller particles and that thus the fixed "point of Archimedes," which manifests the truth and the meaning of existence, must not be sought below by structural analysis of profane science, but above, in the direction of the Author of the work. For in these scientific analyses, the world of matter decomposes in a substance of ever finer grain which slips through the fingers of savants. No response to the "enigmas of life" posed by science is to be awaited from that quarter, and the searchers of our time certainly have motives to agree entirely with the sense in which Nietzsche, the romantic negator, despairingly pronounced his *Umsonst*—"in vain." In the end, the contribution of science only confirms that the truth must be sought from on high.

The symbol, however, is more than a natural manifestation. Religious rites depend upon symbolism. Just as we say that the presence of God in nature is double, spiritual and symbolic, similarly the religious rite is the expression of a presence in the two acceptations. It is not a meaningless phrase to say: "The Lord is in His holy temple." The temple does not only represent, it is the

---

[7]Modern astronomy, moreover, thanks to better instruments, has enlarged its knowledge of the endless world of the stars, and by this fact the Copernican image of the world has become "provincial" and of a limited value.

dwelling place of the divine in the world. The pontifical palace, episcopal ornaments, richly decorated sanctuaries and temples are expressions of the celestial principality—as are the men who act in this display, who are its supports, and who represent it; all this is a question of secondary importance. Whether these men succumb to the temptation of pride and confuse their position of minister with the divine sublimity changes nothing of value in the symbol.

The symbol simultaneously is and represents. It manifests and reflects the divine reality in a direct and vertical fashion. This is why it must be distinguished from allegory which is an analogy in horizontal perspective, therefore indirect. For the symbol is a "here and now" seized intuitively, which reaches us as a bolt of lightning, while allegory is apprehended as a pedagogic and discursive process in space and time. Allegory represents but it "is" not in a spiritual sense.[8]

This ambivalence of the symbol—it is and represents at the same time, it unites essence and existence—makes it even more difficult for contemporary secularized man to grasp, and the same applies of course to the reality which the symbol manifests. The more the cloud cover thickens, which veils the light of truth, the more the symbol loses its meaning in existence. The man of today lives ever more and more in a world of "things," and this diminishes the capacities of perception, the possibilities of which are reduced to the mere domain of the sensorial and the mental, and these he perceives as objectivity. He glories in his growing spiritual impoverishment.

At the same time he cannot dissimulate completely his bitterness and his deception. Nor can he completely forget his origin, and he retains the sentiment of what he has lost due to this secularization. In his smallness and his disappointment, he takes revenge,

---

[8]A symbol, however, can be dissimulated in an allegory. "Suffer the little children to come unto me" is the point of departure of an allegory; it is only as children that one can enter the Kingdom of Heaven; the child is then compared to the innocence that we must have in order to gain eternal life. At the same time the child is effectively and symbolically in possession of a celestial innocence. In a way, the symbol makes the cadre of allegory blaze forth.

though generally in an unconscious manner; he attacks the world of symbols. He literally throws himself on the symbolic world of nature and of ritual. Certainly it has been said of nature that man must reign over her and eat of her fruits. But our Lord has not said that man must destroy nature. The exploitation of nature by secularized man, especially in the industrial age, is a veritable destruction, a blind utilization because it attacks in nature that which is divinely symbolic, its original purity. The exploitation is a blasphemy against the divine, for it is an expression of human egotism and pride. The exploitation and destruction of nature has for motive only the attraction of material gain, and these destructive forces are directed also against man himself. It is this blind exploitation which has given birth to the social category which is perhaps that most to be pitied of any which has ever existed on this earth—the industrial proletariat. And now industry, guided by its instinct of an animal of prey, lies in wait for all natural resources and by its tendency to destroy the environment, stands as a menace over our entire terrestrial life.

The attack against symbolic rituals is no less virulent, but it has other points of departure. In the first place, it takes aim at symbols as if they had been invented by man. It is claimed that the beauty of ritual worship is an expression of human presumption, a manner of masking the image of God in order to substitute man in his illusory and imaginary grandeur. The art of temples, sacerdotal vestments, episcopal palaces, the loftiness and the pomp of prelates, all this is interpreted as expression of human—especially clerical—pride, and the wish to dominate. Within the confines of the Christian world, this attitude attains its maximum in Calvinism which is animated by a resentment that is social in content and of which the outcome is the inverse: man is placed at the center, and major decisions are taken by votings held in democratically organized communities.

Ever since the closure of the gate of the Garden of Eden, man is a fallen creature. He wanders* ever more deeply in a world in which

*Translator's note: The French verb *errer* has the sense of wander aimlessly or stray, as well as that of err or to be misguided.

the attractions constantly cause him to take the wrong directions. Thus he perceives ever more weakly the interior divine voice and the light which should guide him in the darkness. This is why it is ever more difficult to grasp the interior spirituality without which all symbols are devoid of meaning. Consequently, increasing worldliness can make of the symbol a fragile instrument in spiritual conflicts and the passage to inconoclasm may be remarkably short.

The symbol is one of the forms of divine manifestation in the world. The other is revelation. The intellect and revelation are the two sources of human knowledge of God. The one is interior and the other is exterior. Man acquires the one on the essential level and the other on the existential level, but the two have the same origin. Revelation is divine "intervention" in existence. As though lightning flashing from a cloudless heaven, the message descends on a world apparently determined by the forms with which such "interventions"may appear incompatible. If the cosmic symbol reflects the infinite perspective, which in time and space constitutes creation qua stability and harmonious unity, revelation is the accidental fact which suddenly appears in the manifested substance. Like a mirror, the symbol is the horizontal aspect which requires an interpretation and a "translation." Revelation is the vertical aspect, the mediator which speaks directly to man.

The bearers of divine revelation in the world are first of all the *Avataras*, founders of religions which God sends to us and by which He manifests the truth. It is these founders of religions who transmit the truth among men. The prophets of the Old Testament continue the communication of revealed truth, recalling, guiding, warning. In the three great Semitic religions, Judaism, Christianity, and Islam, the revelation is continued in the holy books. In the beginning was the Word, and the Word was made flesh.

But revelation is addressed to a world full of imperfections and of contradictions. A message is first of all limited in space. All the men of the earth are not touched by the unique and same message. Later, the revelation is spread out in time. In paradisiacal existence, intellection and revelation are one; primordial man lives in a center where the dimensions of time and space have no importance. The expulsion from paradise is a dispersion and this is why the correctives supervene, destined for men under the form of revelations varying according to times and places. The alliance concluded with Yahweh by Moses and his people is not independent of prevailing conditions. Nor is the message of Christ independent of the dissolution, in the times of later Antiquity, of cosmic solidarity—hence the emphasis placed by Christianity on personal salvation. The divine message has a concrete character which we should not contest in the vain fear of weakening in it a spirituality that surpasses time and space.

The play of oppositions that characterizes existence does not remain on the exterior of religious life. All our confessional antagonisms, all the theological disputes, and all the wars of religion prove nothing concerning the transcendent and immutable truth. All these struggles only attest that the world is a created work, that the truth is certainly found manifested here, but only "as in a mirror," perfect in its origin, but exteriorized by imperfect men. This is why revelation itself is not exempt from this quandary. It is, then, the more important to conserve, protect, and defend the revealed Word, for all can be corrupted by the hands of men.

It is here that tradition enters. As terrestrial creatures, we are tempted to forget ourselves in speculations and activities. Our religious life easily becomes arbitrary. For the one part, circumstances of occasion, of time and place may determine our religious attitude, and for the other part we may be tempted to confine our religious life within individual arbitrariness. Existence continually changes and individual variations are ceaseless. To situate one's spiritual life in the accidental and individual would in effect be to build on sand. If one had to allow that the constant changes in terrestrial forms and the individual mutations might serve as base for spiritual life, one would inevitably end in confusion and dissolution. By allowing the play of oppositions of terrestrial existence and individul subjectivism to ultimately determine the foundations of spiritual life, without fail one would place this latter under the banners of secularization.

Our religious life is simultaneously interior and exterior. According to certain tendencies of piety, one hopes and one believes that it would be possible for man to lead only an interior life, to follow exclusively an esoteric path. This is a dangerous illusion. There are certainly holy men who have been independent of an exterior order, exoteric and orthodox, but these are exceptions which confirm the rule. This tendency to lead only an interior life is deceitful, principally in that an "interior" deprived of the support of a formal order is open to penetration by psychic influences that lead it to sentimentality and arbitrariness.

We live in the world of forms and the intellective consciousness must be supported by the forms that procure us our religious life. The revealed word must be protected and preserved in its originality. The *intellectus* and revelation certainly are not indestructible things that one can seize like tools and use no matter how. Ignorance, egoism, and wickedness necessitate that the intellective process have a support in exterior life and for revelation, an escort, a vigilant guard so that the message of God may be transmitted in its authenticity to each generation. For each generation must know that the message is true and authentic, and that it is not a product altered by subjectivism and opportunism.

The primary objective of the tradition lies here. This task must be accomplished in the world with its forms and its imperfections. But the source of energy is not in this changing and subjectively lived world, nor in its individual and accidental forms. The form of religious life draws its force from spiritual reality and the presentation of this latter on earth is its formal mission. This is why temples and the objects they contain, the writings and ritual ordinances, possess an interior force, a holiness which must not be attacked or perturbed. This is also why spiritual life in the world presents itself under forms which nevertheless are not of this world, which are not submitted to the variations of that which is accidental or individual. This paradoxical encounter in the world of forms between that which changes constantly and that which remains eternally immutable becomes more and more incomprehensible to contemporary secularized man; and consequently the modern theology of adaptation is always more disposed, in its *aggiornamento*, to turn our regard away from it.

Tradition is a protection and a support. It mounts guard around sacred acts; it defends them from profanation; it sustains, thanks to its cultural and ritual elements, the fragile spirituality of the individual. But the mission of tradition is not exclusively conservation. It is also explanation. Or rather: it is an interpretation in terms, in ideas, and in terrestrial concepts of the message given at the origin. It is at this point, in the religions having sacred Scriptures, that hermeneutics enter, which is the just interpretation of sacred documents, interpretation which always must include penetration in depth of the texts and an elucidation of all the dimensions which these texts contain.

But tradition is not only conservation and interpretation. It is, in the third place, development of what is seed at the origin of the message and which on the terrestrial level must spring up as life and come to maturity. If the divine message to man was a detailed legal text or description of all the duties of human kind, all the plan set forth in the account of creation would be impossible to realize, for the mandate of terrestrial overlordship assigned to a man is a vast mission implying liberty and responsibility. In the sacred, in doctrine, in legislation, in social life—throughout, man must be an active creature endeavoring to pursue the divine work and to represent it in all the measure that earthly imperfection permits.

Thus tradition is somewhat comparable to a tree growing without cease. Starting from a given substratum, the need for prolongations and means of expression increases. A tradition necessarily lives in space and time; this is why, despite its fundamentally conservative character, it is necessary to interpret and develop it. Jesus Christ instituted the Last Supper, but is the sacrament which resulted from it as a traditional development in contradiction with the evangelical message brought by Christ? No one would dare so pretend. Is the cultural richness of the Christian world a falsification of the divine truth? The masses that down through the centuries have constituted the strength of communities of the faithful would give the best lie to such an assertion. The Christian religion does not have a sacred language, but it has at its disposal a rich compensation in the form of Latin, sonorous liturgical language, full of substance.[9]

Thus tradition is at once preservation of the divine truth, interpretation of that truth, and finally the labor of edification in which each stone carries the signature of the Creator, all terrestrial activity conforming to the regency received. To each of these three degrees, however, a question of great importance is imposed: to whom must be confided the mission of preserving, of interpreting, and of pursuing the edification?

There are men who have received from God spiritual gifts which others do not have. It is to them, who have at their disposition superior aptitudes, that the task is given of continuing transmission of truth on earth. The founders of religions and the prophets, apostles, saints, sages and masters of knowledge are endowed with a spiritual richness and a competence which permits them to communicate to us the divine truth, each according to the function which has been given him and according to his own proper vocation. It is these gifts to which 1 Cor. 2:13 alludes: "words not taught by human wisdom but taught by the Spirit, interpreting spiritual truths to those who possess the Spirit."

Even if the reality is contested and denied by the sovereign people's prophets of egalitarianism and the theologians who are their fellow travelers, one must not relax in insisting upon this: there are men who have received from God spiritual gifts superior to those of others, and who by this fact are invested with functions which everyone cannot pretend to fulfill. Tradition is governed, thanks to these spiritual functions assigned by God and not by discussions in popular assemblies.

---

[9]The decision of Vatican II to give the Catholic Church the liberty to use the vernaculars in the liturgy on the pretext that the latter becomes thereby more "comprehensible" for the faithful is a typical and tragic manifestation of the encroachment of secularization even in the religious domain. On the one hand, the divine presence in the Mass is not better seized if the Mass is said in Polish—the divine presence is one thing and our means of verbal expression is something else—and on the other hand it is a remarkable inconsequence for a Church that calls itself Catholic, that is, universal, to surrender to verbal provincialism, the free use of national languages, and this is at a time when ecumenism is imposed as never before.

Finally, we pose one decisive question for the practice of the faith in the modern epoch. How can we reconcile all this with human reason? We have spoken of the intellective and intuitive consciousness of the transcendent truth. We have mentioned symbols, revelation, and tradition. We have said that such were the paths of truth and of life. But what happens if our reason refuses all this? Must we divide our consciousness in two sections, one reasonable and other "irrational"? Are we going to be interiorly distended by the conflict between these two tendencies? Are we going to try to "save our soul" by taking refuge in a *credo quia absurdum.** These questions require responses.

**Credo quia absurdum est,* "I believe it because it is absurd."

Chapter 5
OBJECTIVITY

There are two manners of responding to the question relative to the rapports between reason and religious experience. We can refer to the limits of reason and say that it lacks competence beyond certain limits. We can also say that religion is "something different" from that which pertains to the world of rational thought, and thus we establish a parallel between religion and reason as if it were a question of two orders of incommensurable grandeur.

Neither of these two responses is false, but both are unsatisfactory. Certainly, the transcendent truth cannot be seized by our mental faculties and in our earthly life; nor is it possible to place on the same footing and to mix the truth of which the source is transcendent and that which results from a discursive mental process. But once again: let us suppose that reason refuses religious experience and the teaching to which it is tied. In fact, every religious representation encounters reason at some point. But let us go further. The intellectual consciousness, the intuitive *intellectus*, cannot transmit a message regarding the divine reality without transposing it, with man, into a sensorial and mental consciousness. Assuredly we say that our knowledge of a superior reality is intuitive, but as creatures we must transfer this experience onto the mental level for it to become conscious. The testimony of the divine truth must be manifested in our mortal and psychic organs. Religious experience in the sensory world therefore inevitably comports an encounter with reason.

If the divine reality and with it religious experience manifesting itself to our sensory and mental organs were in contradiction with reason, that would signify that for thousands of years, for uninterrupted generations of pious men, including innumerable sages and learned men—that they would have lived in a terrible state of interior conflict. In their profound piety, they would have been attached to a way of seeing which their reason would not have admitted. The fearful interior conflict that would have resulted must naturally have left visible traces in the history of humanity. Now nothing indicates such a conflict. Even in our "enlightened" epoch men are found who ally the highest intelligence to simple faith, and we do not have the impression that it is especially from among them that psychiatric asylums draw their inmates.

If this conflict has really existed, the history of humanity would have taken quite another turn. Either there would no longer be churches or religious communities on earth, or humanity in its ensemble would have been deranged. No, the conflict between religious consciousness and human reason is an effect of secularization. When the intellectual consciousness is weakened, following upon a growing spiritual pride, this gives a vaster field of action to the rational mental faculties. In the "light" of rationalism, a symbol would appear more and more as an incomprehensible and absurd form. For profane research, the revelations are only "events" of which the historical authenticity is more and more placed in question. One then comes to consider tradition in all its forms as an obstacle emanating from conservatism, a barrier on the way; and teachings proven by the centuries as chains of spiritual slavery.

Thus the triumphal cortege of rationalism sets out. Luciferian forces believe that they offer themselves as light bearers. In reality they take possession of the darkness which is installed when the interior light is weakened. Reason does not bring a new light, for it is a function; and that which is functional cannot be, by itself, a bearer of light and even less a source of light. Reason, *ratio*, pertains to the world of forms and therefore men cannot attain by their rational faculties an absolute truth or certitude. Rational knowledge is separative; it is made of fragments; it can never be assembled in an absolute and incontestable unity. The truths of rationalism are and remain partial truths.

Reason fulfills its loftiest function as long as it is subordinated to intellectual knowledge.* It is then enlightened by the light of truth which shows the way on the terrestrial level. There is no opposition between the intellect, *intellectus*, and reason, *ratio*, as long as the latter submits to our consciousness of a superior and transcendent truth, and as long as it accepts this role as a function of service. Then in our effort to find the way of truth and of life, reason is allied to intellective certitude, to the symbol, to revelation and tradition. One assuredly knows that men, in their earthly imperfection, do not always follow such ways. But one also knows that the light exists and with it the possibilities of guidence. And that is what is decisive. The vices of judges and lawyers do not give us the right to abolish justice, any more than the sins of priests furnish arguments against the existence of God.

The intellectual and rational are both "in man" as means to attain the truth. In a way they provide a setting for the three other means which are symbolism, revelation, and tradition. The symbol is the cosmic reflection of the divine. Revelation is a "here and now" which penetrates the cosmos as a ray of the sun bringing a witness which captivates and preserves us. Finally, tradition constitutes the mode to which we must conform ourselves in order to receive and preserve [these gifts of Heaven]. It guides our efforts destined to guard, to maintain, and to transmit in time and space—that is, on the horizontal plane—that which has come to us vertically as revelation.

Even if the color bearers of the Kingdom of Man are presented under the most modest exterior, saying that they do not pretend to resolve all the enigmas of life, they seek even so to credit themselves with this: in the Kingdom of Man, they say, all approaches to truth are characterized by objectivity, in contrast with religion, which in its human "personal practice," must be taxed with subjectivism. This attachment of the Kingdom of Man to objectivity, one

---

*Translator's note: That is, to *faith*, to adopt the expression of orthodox Catholicism.

furthermore pretends, would be especially the doing of profane science.

Objectivity signifies that there is an object of knowledge observed by a subject. Such is the point of departure of profane science. Science is the relation between the thinking subject and the object "thought," with the task of establishing the objective reality without taking into account subjective needs or desiderata. This implies that, in order to be true and to have a general value, the opinions of the subject must accord with the objects observed. It is only with the condition of this concordance that science can speak of veritable objectivity.

For Descartes, who laid the philosophical foundations of modern science, reality presents itself to us under two parallel forms: spiritual and material. It is the spiritual under the form of human thought that observes matter, and, for Descartes, human thought constitutes at the same time the ontological proof: *cogito ergo sum*, I think, therefore I am. The meditative contemplation of the world is thus the way of objective truth. The *res cogitans* contemplates the *res extensa*. The incessant and methodic action of human thought on surrounding existence leads to a full and entire knowledge of this latter.[10]

This dualism implying a spiritual world and a material world, a thinking subject and an object "thought," constitutes the base not only of speculative science but of empiricism. In this regard Francis Bacon and Descartes have the same point of departure. Lively polemics have arisen over the question of whether objective reality, the truth, can be attained speculatively or by the gathering and empirical observation of material, but a common base remains: it is that thinking and searching man is the bearer of the aspiration to objective truth. The way is then open to scientific positivism which triumphs in the Western world in the following centuries.

---

[10]Nevertheless, Descartes is not content with that. He holds that thought must perfect itself until it attains the infinite and the absolute. Then man will be capable of acquiring the perfection of the divine nature. (Descartes, *Meditations*, collection Le Monde en 10/18 [Paris, 1963], p. 167.)

The Kingdom of Man, however, offers other ways to attain the hoped-for goal, which is the whole and entire truth about a profane world, sought with profane means. One system of thought, especially, arises against positivism, denying that the human mind soars freely over sensory reality, speculating, examining, gathering material and analyzing structures: Marxism. Karl Marx, who was a so-called young-Hegelian, undertook the reversal of Hegelianism: the only reality is not spiritual but material. The spiritual is found to be contained within this material reality and, as an active and dynamic energy in the material world, it is the "reflection" of the latter. Man is producer; he produces and reproduces himself by nourishment and sexual generation; he also produces merchandise and ideas. These latter, the "ideologies," are the faithful reflections of the position of man in the process of material production. The "ideological superstructure" thus reflects the material foundation, the relations of force which rest on the social structures of the world of matter. *Das Ideele ist das im Menschkopf umgesetzte Materielle.**

According to Marx, man lives exclusively in the material world, and he is there as producer. This productive existence is confounded with his social existence. Man is socially integrated. *Der vergesellschaftete Mensch* is a social being and he has no life outside of society. Marx has resolved the dualism characterizing positivist thought which distinguishes between an observant spiritual subject, man, and the object observed, the sensory world. He has sunk the spiritual into the world of matter, declaring that the material alone is real and that the spiritual is immanent therein. The manifestation of the spiritual is made of projections, of reflections of material reality.

From the spatial point of view, Marx has placed man in a material world that has been rendered absolute. But this material world is not an immutable state. Man lives also in time. How does that which is materially spatial behave in relation to time? Marx responded by declaring that the history of humanity is a dialectical

---

*The ideal is the material transposed in the human brain.

"self-achievement of itself." The goddess of history intervenes in the Marxist system which, by this fact, becomes a very different duality from that of "bourgeois" positivism. The Marxist system of thought is a pseudo-metaphysical fantasy when it elevates these two existential categories of time and space to the rank of pseudo-divinities. Marxism is and remains a freakish product without ties to the reality of which it pretends to be the sole valid interpreter.

Positivism and Marxism have one thing in common: the object of their search for truth is sensory existence. But while Marxism, without making the least effort to prove its affirmation, declares that the only reality is the material order, positivism, as a general rule, shies away from these pseudo-metaphysical notions. The method of positivism is different: it excludes the question of final ends. According to John Locke, our duty is not to know everything. If we only learn to order reasonably our ideas and our actions here below, we shall have no need to worry about all that our consciousness cannot attain. Let us begin, therefore, recommends Locke, by examining our own mental resources as well as our possibilities of action. Our mental means cannot go any further, but let us be content with them. Such is the true sense of the considerations of John Locke on human knowledge.[11]

So how can the two, Marxism and positivism, lay claim to objectivity? If Marxism was a faithful image of reality, it would be necessary to explain how the material order could be assured of keeping its preponderance in space, and how history realizes itself in a dialectical way. Who guarantees to these powers, matter and history, their dominant position? Where is the superior authority which forever maintains the supremacy of the world of matter, and what invisible hand historically guides men towards the complete "liberation from need," towards the decisive leap into the "kingdom of liberty"? Marxism does not know the answer, for the only

---

[11]John Locke, *An Essay Concerning Human Understanding*, vol. 1, London, 1812, p. 5. A modern savant, the atomic researcher and Nobel laureate P.W. Bridgeman, expresses a similar opinion: Let us avoid the innumerable questions to which we cannot respond by the means of profane science and rather declare them "devoid of meaning". (P.W. Bridgeman, *The Logic of Modern Physics*, 6th impression, [New York, 1951], pp. 28-31.)

truth of this fantastic system of social redemption is that it has come out of the young-Hegelian brain of the professor of philosophy, Karl Marx.

What pretention to objectivity can the positivists make, who declare that all questions that go beyond the limits of reason are "absurd" and "indifferent"? The human psychic faculties, that "intellectual unity" of which Auguste Compte spoke, must be mobilized to encounter the phenomenal world—but who will guarantee that this encounter will open out on objective knowledge, when a great part of the questions relative to this phenomenal world are already excluded?

If we try to penetrate into the world of matter, we find ourselves constantly in the presence of phenomena which we have to take into account in our daily life and which science unhesitatingly uses as cornerstones in its system. We speak of heat, of electricity, of energy, of life. But what is heat, what is electricity, what is energy, what is life? Science can establish within certain limits the relations between different elements of the phenomenal world. What more can it do? Already at the beginning of this century, scientific researchers believed they could conclude that science was incapable of coming any closer to a knowledge of the reciprocal relations of things and phenomena. It is not even possible to establish with certitude the objectivity of these relations nor can we know anything indubitable as regards their validity for all men and in all times. As for our efforts to isolate these phenomena one from another and to seek to determine the essence of them, these efforts are vain, according to the French mathematician, Henri Poincaré. The knowledge that we are able to acquire of the proper nature of things is, at best, a rough likeness.[12]

The efforts of profane science to acquire a complete and objective image of reality runs up against an inexorable frontier at another point. In the course of the last decades, physics has had an ever growing tendency to consider that a full and complete knowledge of a definite scientific domain could not be attained. If man

[12]Henri Poincaré, *La valeur de la science* (Paris, 1905), pp. 265-76.

had, as Descartes thought, fixed points of observation from which he could "contemplate" the world of matter, the hope might exist of arriving at such a general knowledge of things. If he had at his disposal invariable measuring instruments valid in all circumstances, he might put himself to work with some chances [of success]. But in our created world, the concept of time itself is not manifested as an immutable order of grandeur. The definition of time given by Newton—"Absolute, true, Mathematical Time, of itself and from its own nature flows equally without regard to anything external"—is one of the cornerstones of the edifice of the scientific myth which collapsed only in our days. This is why our terrestrial knowledge is and remains fragmentary and, in our created and imperfect world, these fragments cannot be assembled in a true objective unity.[13]

Profane science essentially builds upon measurements. These are relations between phenomena which may be accessible to observation—not the essence of the phenomena—and this is why profane science is more and more prisoner of the necessity for quantitative verification. Even the behavioral sciences are henceforth dominated by this quantitative preoccupation, as if we could learn anything essential about man by enregistering in statistical compilations his attitudes towards the world which surrounds him. Even though physics may have brought to light the fragility of our mathematical observations, quantitative methods of research continue to develop in profane science.

These ideas about the possibility of reaching some objectivity by means of measurements and observations of the quantitative order are combined with conceptions on the natural relations of cause and effect. At bottom, this notion of causality rests on the opinion according to which phenomena must admit of explanation by preceding events, that the future will be determined by the

---

[13]Bridgeman, *Logic of Modern Physics*, p. 45. Werner Heisenberg (*Dialectica* 3:1 [1948]:333) formulates this situation in these terms: "Was wir mathematisch festlegen, ist nur zum kleinen Teil ein 'objektives Faktum,' zum grösseren Teil eine Uebersicht über Möglichkeiten." (That which we establish mathematically is only in weak measure an "ojective fact," but in much greater measure a glimpse of possibilities.)

present and that the present is determined by the past. This conception of causality, therefore, consists in looking backward; everything that comes to pass is the effect of something in the past (*post hoc, ergo propter hoc*). In this way profane science reckoned on existence as being subordinated to a causal order and therefore dependent on laws. Thereby, also, it has been possible to present "nature" as a root postulate in virtue of which men will be able, on the one hand to explore this "nature" and its intimate "secrets" in conformity with laws and bound to causality, and on the other hand to live in the reassuring conviction of always "being on solid ground."

Even the idea of causality has been revealed as false. When one asked him if causality really existed, the English physicist and Nobel laureate Paul Dirac responded: "sometimes"! He had been obliged, as so many others before him, to recognize that science faces a growing number of questions to which it is incapable of responding. "There is the quantum jump," he said, "and it is quite possible that God acts on it." Max Plank considers that the scientific notion of causality, "efficient causality," must be bound to an inverse relationship of cause to effect, that is to say that existence also tends toward a final objective, "final causality."[14] Thus is recognized the order that Aristotle had clothed in that terminology and which, for the men of the Christian Middle Ages, was a conviction permitting no doubt: it is God who directs the arrow and not, as Occam pretends, the archer. There exists a cause in existence, but the objective reality of this cause must not be sought on earth nor with terrestrial means.

The classical image of the world that profane science had inherited from the seventeenth and eighteenth centuries has been

---

[14]Max Plank, *Religion und Naturwissenschaft, Vortrag in Baltikum* (Mai 1937), 6th ed. (Leipzig, 1938), pp. 26ff. Plank's conclusion is that a certain conformity to laws exists independently of a thinking humanity. There is an existence, a power ruling over the world and there are therefore domains where religion and science meet, declares Plank. That superior power cannot be the object of human knowledge and it is there that the limit of science is situated. This is why religion and science are not mutually exclusive, "sondern sie ergänzen und bedingen einander." (But they complete and are conditioned by one another.)

broken. In reality, this image was much more speculative than was thought by those who for so long had enthusiastically accepted its guidance. It rested on a series of postulates that had no foundation in reality, and one regarded these postulates as "objective" parts of that reality which should itself be submitted to an objective research that derived from what it was necessary to demonstrate. But it appeared that only a small part of the domain of scientific research was accessible to human knowledge, that the instruments and methods utilizable were very insufficient and that a constant variability, principally in time and space, ceaselessly thwarted plans aimed at assuring a fixed and sure point of observation.

But, in the final analysis, what of the first and ultimate instrument that man has at his disposition, his thought? Human thought is an objective process which develops in the dimensions of space and time. It is produced in space in the sense that it is tied, as an operative process, to the physical faculties of each individual. The "flight of thought" is a *licentia poetica* which does not liberate thought from its spatial tie with the individual. The thought is mine; it cannot be given up to another creature. Nor can it be raised up to the point of becoming a universal process.

Thought is, then, an operative process which takes place in the dimension of time. It is a lapse of time, and memory, which preserves and actualizes the past and depends upon it. Creative fantasy also belongs to thought, as well as the capacity to associate and combine materials which, with the aid of memory, is also drawn from time.

By the fact of its ties with time and space, and of its association with the physical and mental capacities of man, thought is "condemned" to be part of the created world. Just as man himself is part of creation, his thought is part of the mental forces active in terrestrial life. This is why thought is and remains a function, an operative faculty within the cadre of all the limits traced for man. It is an operative process of which the efficacy is constantly bumping up against its limits. The capacity of human thought to embrace in its attention, to penetrate and to grasp the problems of the world of things is therefore limited.

By this fact, human thought is also deprived of the capacity of reaching an objective, full and complete knowledge of the reality in which we live. Profane man never attains the essence of things by the operations of his thought. Nevertheless, it is a long way from there to contesting the value of scientific research. The knowledge of relations between phenomena is precious and we do not reject it. That which one calls anti-intellectualism is not only a limited, desperate, and unworthy attitude, it is also a proud refusal of our rational powers which God has given us in order that we might make use of them. That which must be spurned is the pretention of science to the domination of the world of the mind as well as its presumptuous and conceited ambition according to which it and it alone is capable of reaching the source of the truth.

When John Locke affirmed that a pre-rational consciousness, given by God and innate in man, does not exist, he not only denied the *intellectus*. At the same time he enclosed man in subjectivism. For the man of empirical sensualism, of whom Locke is the first messenger in modern times, has refused his faculty of objectification from the moment when he refused to use intellective knowledge and had recourse only to his sensory and mental capacities. With this profane man, all knowledge, every notion, is subjective. For thought cannot think itself; it cannot scrutinize the tenor of truth of the products that it elaborates qua instrument.

It is in our intellective consciousness that we experience the truth, and in the "eye of the heart" that we objectify it. We "contemplate" the truth, not by a logical and discursive process, nor as the final result of an experiment or of an empirical gathering of material. We "contemplate" the truth in the *light* of which the Gospels speak. The world is reached by solar rays of truth, and this is why man must know the true nature of the world. Thereby we experience objectivity and truth as essentially the same thing: the true is objective and the objective is true.

Consequently, the circle of objectivity is closed. As a creative wave, the world is object for the divine truth. But that which is objective is not passive acceptance; this is not a knowledge or a notion that we can classify in archives. The truth is infinitely more than a question of wisdom. Truth is also life. A life in the truth must be lived in the way of the truth. Far beyond biological life and its limited preoccupations is the life of which the Gospels speak: "And the life was the light of men." The light guides and, in the objective intelligence which we have at our disposal thanks to the light, we try to attain the source from which all proceeds. Union with the Creator, power which dominates all things, is the goal. Objectivity and subjectivity, this polarization of created existence, is extinguished in reunion. This is why there is no wisdom higher than this: "I am the way, the truth, and the life."

Chapter 6
GOOD INTENTIONS

In the Kingdom of Man, the mundane secular search for the truth rests on an argumentation which bears a strong moral imprint. Even if one may doubt the possibility of finding the full and entire truth by profane ways, even if in this profane search for the truth it is found impossible to attain that which is objective and absolute; nevertheless, it is declared, all these efforts are characterized by an honest and courageous quest for the true. It is our duty, Descartes tells us, to give an account of our progress in human learning, without concealing anything. If I have found anything which implies scientific progress, Descartes continues, I must not conceal it.[15]

Profane scientific research will thus be led with a nonchalance which has, in appearance, the mark of a noble passion for the truth. One must follow the scientific ways of truth even if they lead to the gates of Hell. All the results of research must be put at the disposal of humanity. To suppress the results of research or an invention is the equivalent of joining the partisans of obscurantism. Nevertheless, even at its beginnings, European science allowed its pragmatic character to appear. The principal objective of the Kingdom of Man is to make the human being the custodian of power on

[15]René Descartes, *Discours de la Méthod (Paris, 1962), pp. 61ff.*

earth, and one of the most important means to reach this goal is science. It is for this reason that science is in the first place at the service of the appetite for power, and Descartes himself has clearly indicated his orientation in affirming that the mission of science is to "promote the common good." This pragmatic orientation of modern science constitutes at the same time the base of its moral existence: enhance the physical and psychic well-being of men, and lead mankind "forward."

Science thus becomes one of the most powerful instruments of the Kingdom of Man. But, from the fact of its pragmatic—and consequently moral—orientation, the requirements of truth cease to be essential. It is a question of exploring the world of things, in such a manner as to procure to man the means of dominating this world. Knowledge is power, declared Francis Bacon. At the same time there are opened to man the possibilities of enjoying without reserve all that the world can offer to its dominator. Henceforth, all that is "beyond" seems ever less interesting, and the speculations of profane science on this subject seem as "unnecessary," as "useless." Let us occupy ourselves therefore with what is accessible to the rational creature, opines John Locke, and let us not be importuned by certain things that escape our knowledge.[16]

From this pragmatic point of departure, profane science lands in the bog of existentialism and, on this moving terrain, the scientist defines himself as at once humble, honest, and courageous in his search for the truth. He believes himself humble because he knows how fragile and incomplete are the results of all research. He believes himself honest because he considers that he is not bound by any pre-rational notion and therefore thinks he pursues his activity without preconceived ideas. He believes himself courageous because he does not fear unveiling disagreeable things before men. On the other hand the defenders of religion are presented as

---

[16]"Our business here is not to know all things, but those which concern our conduct. If we can find out those measures whereby a rational creature, put in that state in which man is in this world, may, or ought to govern his opinions, and actions depending thereon, we need not to be troubled that some other things escape our knowledge." (John Locke, *An Essay Concerning Human Understanding*, vol. 1, p. 5.)

"enemies of the light" who, in a sterile and life-negating manner, entrench themselves behind dogmatic and orthodox systems. At the same time the defenders of the faith are accused of being cowards who are afraid of the light; they are taxed with pride and presumption because they persist in demanding the recognition of an absolute and transcendent truth. Subsequently profane science, to which one simultaneously attributes the humility of a servant and the heroism of a Prometheus, can appear as responsive to all the moral exigencies posed by the current system of values in the Kingdom of Man.

This attitude in the search for the truth, apparently so courageous and at the same time so totally pragmatic, extends its effects well beyond the domain of strictly scientific investigation. In modern society, power and well-being, with the principles of force and desire, are the targets at which all thought, all action and all aspiration are aimed. Opinion may be divided on the means of reaching these objectives. The consequences of our actions may be miserable. Nevertheless, even if all that is as imperfect and deceitful as possible, we are assured that all these efforts are stamped with "good intentions." It is thus that one pretends to bring a moral legitimization to the color bearers of the system and to their epigones.

But there is more. The subjects of the Kingdom of Man are also relieved of responsibility. Popular sovereignty implies that one cannot exact responsibility from anyone other than the holder of power; that is, precisely, the people. But the people cannot accuse themselves, and cannot themselves condemn themselves. A holder of power is a sovereign, and the latter cannot condemn himself to prison. He can only accuse and condemn him who transgresses the laws and ordinances of the sovereign. And only he can be brought to justice who infringes and transgresses the laws and ordinances emanating from the popular sovereignty.[17] As for the people itself,

---

[17]Here is to be found the psychological explanation of the fact that all the regimes which are not founded on the principle of popular sovereignty are presently fought so violently, while the most frightful massacres committed "in the name of the people" by the regimes called the people's democracies do not incur any blame.

composed of loyal subjects of the Kingdom, it is free of responsibility. They have only to enjoy the glorious irresponsibility of their power, "for thine is the kingdom, and the power and the glory." The dance around the golden calf can continue uninhibited. One must have one's part in the banquet of life, lead the "good life" here and now. No one will ask us for an accounting nor make us assume responsibilities. This irresponsibility is a fantastic means of seduction at the disposal of the Kingdom of Man. Who is opposed to all these seductions? Who is charged with the heavy burden of responsibility?

Normative values are eliminated, eternal truths are jeered at, the blade of the guillotine falls noisily, and the revolutionary committees of "public safety" devise new ways for the "liberation" of humanity. Nothing must hold back these "good intentions" from realizing happiness on earth. The future is a "progress" unlimited by any horizon and where no one will incur any responsibility, because the day of Judgment is denied. The problem of truth is more and more thrust to the rear for the sake of the moral and, behind this latter, pragmatic justification. Attention is ever more turned away from notions of truth and falsehood to be directed towards that which is profitable to man. By this diversion, interest more and more attaches itself to terrestrial things and is limited to the world of sensible phenomena. That which serves to qualify intentions proceeds from the terrestrial and tangible domain, and this domain defines good as that which favors sensory well-being.

By this substitution of morally justified profane aspirations in the place of the problem of truth, the Kingdom of Man gains several advantageous positions. Its profound objectives which are the practice of an egoism without fetters and the possibility for the man devoted to his own self-interests, of "realizing himself"—these objectives are dissimulated by a moralizing mask and receive a "superior" legitimization: it is stated that it is not a question of egoism, but of good, and it is this good which must be offered to the inhabitants of the earth. This dissimulation permits the presentation of subjective egoism as disinterested and objective aspiration. In the face of this even the religious front vacillates. Many of those who pretend to represent the Kingdom of God and His justice are not only disposed, for example, to see in atheistic communism a system proceeding from a good thought and from an "elevated ideal"; numerous, also, are those who accept peace and collaboration with this system, for it is stated that the "aspiration to the good" is a factor for union and opens the way to this collaboration.[18]

Under the aegis of popular sovereignty and drawing support from "good intentions" and their moral justification, there is presently developing in the Kingdom of Man a dream-like and utopian movement which stands in lively contrast to the objectivity which is supposed to hold sway there. Thomas More knew that his Utopia was just that; it was a "mirror for princes" in which the monarchs of the baroque era could have the image of an ideal order and compare it with the lamentable conditions prevailing in their States. This utopian ideal was not meant to be translated into fact. On the other hand, the political, social, and technocratic dreamers of our time believe that the utopias of today will be the reality of tomorrow.

How is it possible to be so far removed from reality? Certainly, the pseudo-religious needs of contemporary society are enormous, but how can the critical sense be put aside with so much insistence as one sees in our era? Here one can discern an interesting duality in the administration of the system. The course of secularization progresses according to two great currents, rationalism and sentimentalism. Cut off from the living sources of transcendent truth, incapable of objectifying the world in which we live in the light of the *intellectus*, secularized man is reduced to his mental faculties—principally reason and sentiment. But it is not a question of two

---

[18]One should remind the contemporary partisans of *aggiornamento* of what Meister Eckhart said in these words: "Nun könntest du fragen, *wann* der Wille ein rechter Wille sei? Dann ist der Wille vollkommen und recht, wenn er ohne jede Ich-Bindung ist und wo er sich seiner selbst entaussert hat und in den Willen Gottes hineingebildet und geformt ist." [Now you could ask *when* the will is a true will. The will is complete and right when it exists without any ego attachment and where it has given up itself and has formed itself into the will of God.] Meister Eckhart, *Deutsche Predigten und Traktate* (Munich, 1955), p. 54.

domains really separate from one another. It would be insupportable to live exclusively in the glacial world of rationalism. It would be equally unbearable in a condition in which sentiment could eliminate every reasonable thought. This is why reason and sentiment are so often mixed and why they interpenetrate one another so intimately that it is frequently impossible to know what stems from the one or the other.

This is inevitable. Rationalism and sentimentalism follow one another as the shadow follows the body. It is chimerical to imagine that thought proceeds in the clear light of rationalism in a march that is "pure" and free of any sort of "dross." The discursive operations of thought have as integral parts memory, imagination, and sentiment. A thought without any preconception, unconditioned and objective in the Cartesian sense therefore does not exist. In this regard modern society is incapable of organizing itself in a reasonable fashion, for it gives no purchase to opposing views. When the intellective data is rejected and denied, there no longer exists any possibility of objectivation or of examination of the truth.

The system is reduced to a subjectivism in which two currents, rationalism and sentimentality, mingle their waters. How could it be otherwise? For the one part, the Kingdom of Man entertains the idea that it is a question of establishing a world that is objective, scientifically controlled, sober, and founded on real facts. On the other hand, its prophets make use of sentimentality to muddle up everything and raise a false warmth that one declares to be justice, love of men, good will, and good intentions.

This is the double play that leads the system to the highest level. One speaks with disdain of the superstition of the Middle Ages. In reality, men were then much more objective and conscious of real facts than are our contemporaries. In the modern era, and thanks to secularization, superstition and credulity have seized such an influence in society as they never had before. In the social, political, philosophical, and pedagogical spheres rational and sentimental tendencies have been intermingled since the epoch called—with very little reason—the "century of light." Man, devoted to his own self-interests, passes himself off not only as a philosopher, but also as economist and reformer of society by virtue of physiocracy, utilitarianism, and liberalism. All the world of thought, complicated and full of contradictions, of which Rousseau is the great prophet, is only a dazzling amalgam of two blind beliefs: in reason and in sentiment. But occultism and superstitions of the most varied kinds were also to be found in the spiritual escort of the French Revolution, all in violent contrast to the adored rationalism.[19]

In the nineteenth century there arose popular social and political movements which, at the same time as the "low church" sects, impregnated society with the poisoned mix that Rousseau had made of sentimentalism and rancorous rationalism, aiming particularly at the traditional elements that still bore the mark of hierarchy. This is the same epoch that saw the birth of Marxism, and it is a notable sign of the reigning confusion of our days that this doctrine, with its grotesque mixture of materialism and historical metaphysics, should show such a renaissance since World War II.

One of the most important characteristics of Western development in the course of the last two centuries is the uninterrupted growth of sentimentalism. Rationalism combines with an ever stronger dose of self-pity before the hard conditions of existence. Fear and suffering are stigmatized as hostile forces creating obstacles to the "happiness" of man. Instead of aspirations for the establishment of a reasonable order determining human relations on the social and political level are substituted movements of which the principal incentive is hatred of the "interior enemy." And the wave of secularization always flows in its two great currents, rationalism and sentimentalism, this latter assuming ever greater amplitude. Marked at the same time by self-pity and by conceit,

---

[19]One will find a suggestive and frightening image of the reigning intellectual confusion in the "century of lights" in the work of Paul Hazard, *La Pensée Européen au XVIIIme siècle de Montesquieu à Lessing*, 1-2 (Paris, 1946). See also Bernard Fay, *La Franc-Maçonnerie et la révolution intellectuelle du XVIIIme siècle* (Paris, 1935), and Pierre Trahard, *Les Maîtres de la sensibilité française au XVIIIme siècle (1715-1789)*, 1-3 (Paris, 1931-1932), to note only some of the current great works on the subject.

secularized man goes his way. He believes that in his march he has at his disposal a moral justification: "good intentions."

Who, in the final analysis, permits one to determine which actions are good? Who, facing the continual choices of our daily life, must be there and discern which intentions are truly the good ones? The response in the Kingdom of Man, can only be this: men themselves. It is therefore by public opinion polls and by plebiscites that the leaders acquire data on what may be called good and on the measures considered conducive to that good. It is necessary now to follow the quantitatively determined way which leads to human "happiness"; it is necessary to "give to the people what they want." "Good intentions," conforming to quantitative norms, must be translated into facts and this adaptation takes place in feverish activity and by a labor of reform without respite. The system places us here in the presence of its tragic and vicious circle: in a circular movement of agitation, secularized man believes he reaches reality, and that it is here that the "meaning of life" resides, and that it is here that he must attain his happiness.[20]

If in their effort towards an *aggiornamento*, an adaptation to "reality," the defenders of religion admit this kind of "good intentions," they lend themselves to a game whose rules will not have been conceived and determined by them, but by secular interests and motives. They will ascertain then that modern society is not composed of seditious pagans. On the contrary, the profane world is overabundantly armed with moral motivations and with systems of justice elaborated by the manufacturer of ideological arms. It is this which is taking place in the Kingdom of Man and an *aggiornamento* implies, *nolens volens*, the obligation to adapt oneself.

But there is more. The defenders of the faith are also in the presence of instruments of power, of which the chief is the State.

[20]With his irony at once sweet and bitter, Robert Musil has described this situation in these terms: "Wenn unaufhörlich etwas geschieht, hat man leicht den Eindruck, das man etwas Reales bewirkt." (When something happens without stopping, one easily has the impression that one is producing something real.) Robert Musil, *Der Mann ohne Eigenschaften* (Hamburg, 1952), p. 456.

The growing power of the State, notably, has as effect that the State takes charge of all that which had been, for the adherents of religion, the field of numerous activities in the service of Christian charity. The social State, literally, tears the arms from the hands of the defenders of the faith. Not only does it occupy ever more extended domains of social protection; the modern State is also creator, administrator, and bearer of every right. It is the State that gives the first and the last response to every question relative to social justice. It absorbs power in all domains and above it there is no appeal.

That which had been a community disposing vast possibilities for administering itself and of regulating human relations no longer exists. A right to an opposition to the State in the medieval sense is out of the question, for the omnipotent State reposes on the principle of popular sovereignty. Governments can change; parliaments can adopt defective or blameworthy laws; the State remains nonetheless a functional expression of the sovereign People. The State is "thy" State.

In this State emanating from popular sovereignty, the Hegelian principle of "that which comes to pass is just," in fact, reigns. And when the defenders of religion intervene in the world with their "good intentions" and in the context of their *aggiornamento*, seeking to solidly anchor their faith and their preaching, it is also the State that they run up against. They find themselves confronting a totally atheistic power which obeys no superior directive and which therefore cannot have either good or bad intentions. The State is an apparatus and it is not reasonable to imagine that it may allow itself to be impregnated with a message of Christian morality. Christian communities have existed, but Christian States do not exist and will never exist.

The moral conflicts of humanity are incessant, and moral imperfection is also a part of existential imperfection. We cannot abolish the contradictions in things by reforms. And if one asks us if good intentions and good actions exist, then we will reply, yes and no. All actions are imperfect because they are tied to existence. There are, nevertheless, good actions inspired by good will and by good intention. But what is it that legitimizes the goodness of our will and of our action? If our will and our intention are enlightened by a superior reality, if our will is in submission to that of God and of Providence, then, as Meister Eckhart said, it no longer depends on our "me," that is, on egoism; then our will and our intentions are good.

The important thing is not our actions nor our works, however positive their effects may be on the terrestrial well-being of men. We all live in communities having social imperfections, but one cannot find there a legitimization of permanent revolution. A regime that is profoundly unjust from the point of view of social ethics can be replaced by a bolshevik system under the sign of perfect equality and atheism. To one injustice, then, another succeeds. No one contests that the construction of roads, industrialization, and organization of social welfare have developed in Tibet, but the abolition by Chinese bolsheviks of Tibetan theocracy remains one of the greatest spiritual crimes of our times.

Chapter 7
CONCERNING PREJUDICES

Just as animals have a system of instincts permitting them to protect themselves as well as their progeny, man has at his disposal a mental equipment of an instinctive character. As with animals, the instinctive life of man is aimed at his protection; but, unlike animals, man has infinitely more to protect than his life and the lives of his children in the struggle for existence.

Instinctive behavior is not determined by considerations of a rational order. It does not depend on reasoning and calculation. Instinctive behavior, instinctive acts, may be confirmed after the fact by reason and experience; but their motivation is not of the same nature. Moreover, this instinctive tendency to protection extends well beyond the biological defense of one's own person. Our instinctive disposition includes all creation, the cosmic equilibrium and the preservation of nature in its original purity.

As men, and thanks to our spiritual endowment, we can intervene in the created order, change it and transform it, upset the equilibrium and cause great damage. This exploitation of nature can, over the long run, lead to ruptures of such profound imbalance that our entire existence on the earth is placed in danger. The triumph of industry and technology in the world, from which results a situation which directly menaces our terrestrial life, tragically illustrates the possibility of catastrophic consequences which risk leading to the predominance of spiritual pride over the instinct for the conservation of primordial nature and of cosmic equilibrium.

The instinct of protection does not concern man only as a biological creature, and the natural environment which furnishes him his means of existence. Man must also protect his soul. If the interior equilibrium of the forces of the soul is broken, that may open the door to an autodestruction which cannot be dispositive to a healthy biological existence. Inversely, the forces of the soul may be in a suitably favorable state that an harmonious development seems assured, but exterior disturbances and damage may result in interior disorders. That may be produced if the milieu and the conditions necessary for a healthy development of the soul are compromised or destroyed.

Instinct is assuredly a psychic instrument for holding one's own, but it has more profound roots. Instinctive—or intuitive—capacity has its source in our intellective consciousness of a superior reality. It does not lead us, therefore, to act blindly. It dictates a comportment which can even be translated and take form in thought and opinions. It is there that we have to do with the instinctive or intuitive capacity in its concrete and manifested form, preconceptions or prejudices. As its name indicates, prejudice is a taking of position, an opinion that is not founded upon a decision of our mental faculties, such as reason. Prejudice is prerational; it involves a choice that we take before a rational examination. It is determined by an intuitive certitude and by an instinctive aspiration to which we cannot assign motives in rational terms.

Prejudice [or preconception] wants to defend and preserve the created work on all levels and in all respects. Two points of view are determinant in this regard: it is a question, first, of preserving creation, as well as the truth, in their original purity; and, secondarily, of maintaining a neutralizing equilibrium in all the oppositions of existence on one level and in a superior sense. The first of these tendencies has a vertical aspect, the second a horizontal aspect.

All life in society reposes on a foundation of rules, of norms, and of values which cannot be submitted to revision, and even less can they be destroyed. Above man there resides an order, or a system of principles, which draws its imperative force from a transcendent source. The social order, with all its imperfection, is a reflection on an inferior level of the harmonious unity of the created.

In his active life, man has a single objective: to preserve the life which has been given us, and in this effort, to protect at the same time the life which has been given to all existence. The work of man has no meaning and comports no lasting satisfaction unless it is accomplished in homage to Him who has given us life. In all healthy human working life, therefore, there must intervene an element of prejudice having the function of guardian against destructive forces.[21]

Life in common in society and at work is the activity of adult and mature men. It is an encounter in varying circumstances and at different levels, an encounter marked by oppositions and conflicts. Nothing can be easier than utilizing all these antagonisms to create social chaos. It is always an easy and quickly accomplished task to break up, to disturb, and to demolish. Human communities have been able to exist through thousands of years because they were founded upon an order, the source of which was the divine order itself. It was also possible to transmit these rules and norms from generation to generation. Each time that one tried, with the aid of rational arguments, to place this order in question, the intuitive consciousness of the dependence of this order on divine truth reacted, and this defensive reaction took the concrete form of prejudice.

---

[21]There is not, in our industrial era, any falsification of reality or of nostalgia yet to be seen in agriculture, "foster mother," the form of human activity remaining closest to the cosmic process of creation. In the seasonal alternation of vegetation, in sowing, ripening, and harvest, all creation is represented. This is why in the most highly industrialized countries the menace against agriculture and against cultivators is also a menace against all that which is still healthy and preservative of society in today's world.

The family is the smallest entity in the social life of man. It is the base cell of social life; it constitutes the microcosm, the "atom" of life in common. It is a society in miniature and it contains potentially all that which makes up a sound life in society. The family is a community of comsumption and production, constituting thus the smallest common denominator of human activity.

It is also in the family that are engendered and born the new generations which grow and are raised under the protection of the parents. These latter thus become the terrestrial image of the loving fatherhood of the Creator and they are situated like him "above" their production in the protective and educative function for their children. To this vertical perspective corresponds the horizontal level which is that where love unites the parents and fraternity the children. The family is a microcosmic form of the entire creation.

If we compare the family to the parent cell of the community or to a social atom, we can also say that it contains a nucleus of an atom; it is the point of intersection between the horizontal and the vertical perspectives. It is there that the generations meet, there that is crystallized what tradition comprises with relation to time and space. In time, it is an encounter between the old and the new generations; in space, it is that of the forms of common life which the family knows under its several aspects. This point of intersection thus becomes the point of terrestrial encounter of the two branches of the Christian cross: meeting between heaven and the earth.

The defense of the familial order is a question of life and death for a healthy human cohabitation. In this regard one can refer to an experience extending over millenia, or one can appeal to reason and rely on scientific inquiries. But that carries little weight when the prophets of the system beguile and entice with the aid of promises relative to a human "development" aimed at a world of "liberties" without conflicts, which is only another way to embroider irresponsibility. One also notes that the results of scientific inquiries supporting the familial order are gladly left in the corner and forgotten. In these conditions the principal defense of the family takes the form of prejudice which, here again, constitutes a solid rampart.

The role of prejudice as the most efficacious means of defense of human life on earth stands out more clearly and more completely when, after social and family conditions, we consider those of the individual. Because the individual remains the most vulnerable. It is against him that the forces of destruction are unleashed in the first place and that they register their first successes. Man is especially vulnerable in that he may be isolated and, as an isolated creature, he is often abandoned without succor. This is why the individual must be integrated in the created order in such a way as to be protected and not crushed. For that he must possess, existentially, two conditions: the knowledge of his identity and the appurtenance to a community.

It is only in the intellective consciousness and thanks to the interior light coming from the *intellectus* that we can come to a consciousness of our identity. We have thereby a connection with the source of creation; we have a consciousness of our immortal soul as well as the capacity to objectify our surrounding reality. By the consciousness of the superior *me* which we bear in ourselves, we also have the possibility of experiencing ourselves as personal entities, and it is this which gives us the strength to maintain and harmonize our mental resources.

Man does not, however, possess from his birth interior resources developing by themselves. In the spiritual and mental sense, he does not have an innate nature such as would suffice him to abandon himself to a "self-realization." Ideas on the pretended adaptations of man which are achieved by themselves appertain to a world of fantastic speculation. In order that our consciousness of identity can develop on the earthly level, a process of personal maturation is necessary. But this cannot be produced in a vacuum. An adult and mature milieu is necessary to make a young creature reach the maturation required for the acquisition of a veritable consciousness of identity.

Only the family can offer sufficient stability and durable solidity to realize the process of maturation. It is within its bosom that the children can find themselves in the presence of mature beings, the parents. These latter alone possess the qualities necessary to the process of maturation: love, patience, and responsibility. There is then an encounter marked by tensions and controversies between two partners, the one mature and strong, the other weak and growing. In this encounter, maturation becomes a trial of strength at the same time as a striving towards an objective, which will be the ideal state of the fully and totally mature being. This process has the effect, equally, of drawing more sharply the profile of the personality. The consciousness of a *me* distinct from other creatures follows upon the state of childish symbiosis.

A need for solidarity is added to consciousness of identity. The created work is a world of forms, and it is therefore separative. Created things are distinct from one another, but at the same time they constitute a unity. Every human being is an individual for himself, but his separativity is accompanied by the coexistence of other human creatures. Psychologically as well as biologically, we are created in such a way that we cannot live without solidarity with other creatures. Solitary confinement, or the total isolation of the individual, is an absurdity. A man in such a situation will not only come down with psychological disturbances but will become mentally ill.

The individual finds solidarity first in the family and that on the biological, hereditary, psychological, and social levels. It is in this fundamental entity that each new generation comes to maturity and, with his consciousness of identity, forms his first experience of social solidarity. By virtue of being biologically and psychologically adult, as an active professional man, and as citizen, the human being develops in relation to life in society. Thus we live on three levels, as individuals, as members of a family, and as social creatures; and in our terrestrial life we cannot exclude one of these three levels, which are organically interdependent. If the individual weakens, all the common life is placed in danger. If familial bonds are destroyed, the consequences are disastrous for the individual as well as for society. If social solidarity is broken, there will be baleful repercussions for the family and for the individual.

The consciousness of identity does not, therefore, fill a void. We must have someone or something to objectify our identity, for, like all things in earthly life, identity is a concept of relation. It is only in the solidarity presupposing a process of maturation that we acquire the consciousness of our individual particularity. Our identity then is also experience of our solidarity. This is why identity and community are intimately tied one to the other. The one cannot exist without the other. This enables us to understand why the atomist theory of liberalism relative to the free individual is so false and so devastating. We are now harvesting the fruits, notably (which is paradoxical) under the form of symbiotic behavior—that deadly composite of insufficient personal maturity and of psychic disorder. These two extremes, atomism and symbiosis, arise as the final products of the Kingdom of Man and of his refusal to listen to the voice of wisdom.

The prophets of the system have ceaselessly depicted, in their promises, a land in which tropical vegetation would bloom, where man had only to install himself to have his part in the banquet of life, where he could love and hate without reserve or approbation, and where he could enjoy the delights of power; but it must be noted, this would be a power without responsibility! In the long run, who could turn men aside from all these delectations?

And yet, these prophets find themselves face to face with an obstinate enemy, the force of conservation which persists in fighting long after the ecclesiastical and theological authorities have begun to lay down their arms. This force, this superior notion of a certitude intuitively in our possession and which we manifest in its terrestrial form, is prejudice. For the Kingdom of Man, it is a question of its most dangerous enemy.

In principle, contemporary secularized man impugns every form of prerational knowledge. That not only implies that the human being is less well armed than the animals, the instinctive equipment of which cannot be contested. It signifies, at the same time, that the only valid conception of the true and the just would be founded on sensory experience and rational examination. And this amounts to a proclamation of subjectivism. One does not any longer recognize any superior and universally valid truth. Nothing will count any more but individual conceptions as well as the decisions taken by majorities of voters, decisions moreover which new votes can annul at any moment.

The base of the system is thus posed: it is a sensory order where man constitutes the dynamic center of existence and is the unique interpreter of reality. Nothing is above him, neither norm nor law. For as Rousseau affirms, that which is supreme is not law, but the legislating will. To that he adds another doctrine: by nature man is good and has the means to live according to this goodness. How can that be? By education, responds Rousseau, and he introduces into his philosophy of education an extremely important principle: it is in making man a strong being, liberated from all repressive bonds, norms, and authoritarian constraints that one permits him to achieve the innate goodness in his nature. "All wickedness comes from weakness; the child is naughty only because he is weak; make him strong, he will be good; he who is capable of everything will never do wrong."[22] Obedience, all servile situations, all recognition of a superior power or of a superior truth are therefore, according to this philosophy, sources of wickedness.

Thus the inhabitants of the Kingdom of Man will be strong and their strength will render them free, happy, and good. In fact, the nineteenth century saw some initial and promising successes: the progress of science, social movements, material and technological development, the growth of popular instruction, long periods of peace—all that could give the conviction of being on the right path.

Serious reverses, however, followed with the twentieth century. If the first World War was a terrible shock for all those who had let themselves be lulled to sleep by the progressive optimism of the epoch, the postwar period, with all its reaction culminating in the second World War, was a trial still more grave. In spite of popular instruction, in spite of the liberation from traditional bonds and norms, in spite of all the proud proclamations announ-

---

[22]J. J. Rousseau, *Oeuvres completes* 7 (Aux Deux-Ponts, 1972), pp. 79ff.

cing that henceforth man is master on earth where he makes civic and democratic relationships prevail, in spite of all that, movements of opposition and cells of resistance arise, contradicting and combatting the doctrines of liberty and equality of the system. The political, social, technological, and scientific revolutions have not sufficed. Then what to do?

One notes the existence of a domain where the enemy has not yet been brought down and from whence come the forces of resistance to the progressivist ideal. There are in man interior forces which seek to make truths and superior norms as well as principles of authority prevail, and which proclaim and defend these norms. In brief, it is a question of prejudices. They must, therefore, be annihilated.

On this subject, the study that is most complete and the most invested with authority is the bulky *Studies in Prejudice*[23] published in the United States after World War II. What we find in it is an analysis of the concept of prejudice. This monumental work does not contain a single attempt at explanation or of systematic description of the thing that must be destroyed. In place of that we are presented with an image of man which is an unbelievable *mélange* of the romanticism of nature *à la* Rousseau, of social anthropology shaded with radicalism, as well as Marxist and psychoanalytical lines of argument. There is never explicit adhesion to any of these schools, but one is faced with a consistent procedure of mixing these different systems of thought in order to utilize certain elements of them. Even if it is not clearly expressed, one perceives the opinion that a form of social revolution is inevitable in order to suppress the "authoritarian man" with his tendency to think and act in function of prejudices. But these social, or socialist, upsets will not suffice. They must be accompanied—and here is the central fact—by a psychic upheaval which has to be accomplished by means

---

[23]The part of the work that is most interesting from the point of view of principles is volume 3, by T. W. Adorno, Else Frenkel-Brunswik, Daniel J. Levinson, and R. Newitt and Sanford: *The Authoritarian Personality* (New York, 1952).

of information aimed at extirpating from the mentalities of men the last vestiges of prejudice.

The initial idea is that man does not possess any prerational knowledge. It follows from this that prejudice is a secondary psychic phenomenon, the fruit of traditional, doctrinal, and institutional encroachments upon the conceptual world of men. It is then a relatively easy task, so one deems, to extirpate these pernicious prejudices by fundamental changes in social, political, cultural, and religious structures, by pedagogical reforms and by interventions in the psychism of men.[24]

We are not told what prejudice is, but there are so many the more instructions on its supposed ravages. The traditional, hierarchic, and authoritarian order which has been perpetuated even up to our epoch rests on the recognition of a superior power, and it is this which makes man weak; and if man is weak, he is wicked, or so one thinks in the wake of Rousseau. The weakness of the self engenders anxiety, and anxiety in its turn gives rise to aggressive acts. Weak aggressiveness, anxious and wicked, then seeks to compensate for its painful situation by exercising on others according to the model, "the cat on the mouse and the mouse on the cord." Thus the maleficent system is maintained: enclosed in their neurotic confusion and simultaneously full of sadomasochist enjoyment, these pitiful creatures defend this order of things. They defend that which in reality degrades them, one thinks, for they are entangled in their prejudices. If he liberates himself from these latter as from all authoritarian power, man is promised that he will become a free creature, strong and harmonious. Soundly conscious of his own value, henceforth he will act with a personal responsibility that also permits him to show tolerance towards others. Moreover, man free of prejudice will be happy; and this happiness he will find equally in erotic love, for it is believed that *eros* signifies harmony and peace

---

[24]A representative expression of this way of envisaging things and of the hopes that are placed in these avenues are to be found in a separate work published later, by Max Horkheimer, editor-in-chief of the work cited above: *Ueber das Vorurteil* (Cologne and Opladen, 1963).

with one's neighbors, contrary to the fascist man who, from the fact of his prejudices, is marked by fear and the desire to destroy.[25]

There it is—how this free and happy man will see the light of day! Locke and Rousseau, Marx and Freud have convened an immense ecumenical gathering with the aim of realizing this plan. What are the enemy fortresses that must be attacked and destroyed? There are three, essentially: religious and ecclesiastical orthodoxy, traditional family life, and national and ethnic patriotism. How are they going to be destroyed? Obviously, it is affirmed that it is a question only of eliminating the "authoritarian" spirit, of eliminating from religion, the family and patriotism the "prejudices" that they retain.

Here, sharply clarified, appears the dishonesty of all this program of reforms. A belief in God that is not confident submission to the divine omnipotence is a complete absurdity. Likewise a family life without respect for nor obedience to the parents leads to disintegration. And it is equally unbelievable that a national or ethnic solidarity can be maintained at the same time that one proclaims a "tolerance" aimed at establishing a vulgar promiscuity.

It must be noted that the three fortresses of our prejudices correspond precisely with the three levels on which man finds his identity and his solidarity, where he can live as the creature to whom God has confided the mission of administering the terrestrial world: as individual, as member of a family, and as a social being. The individual attains his veritable personality in the light of the divine truth; and if there exists in our life a relationship of authority, it is that which we have with our Creator. The family is the fundamental cell of all common life, it is the base of the human maturation process, and it constitutes above all else a place of worship where the divine Word is transmitted with the education of new generations. Finally, society, this material, cultural, professional, civic, linguistic, and ethnic community, is the superior form of these relations for the individual as well as for the family.

---

[25]T. W. Adorno and other authors cited, pp. 872, 976, and passim.

A world without frontiers ends in chaos, just as does an erotic life outside a family context. An individual, without roots in a family and in a society, and without direction by the divine Word, is deprived of identity and thence given up to a disarray that can provoke serious troubles in his psychic equilibrium. It is then that our prejudices accomplish their vital work of defense. It is then, also, that the prophets of the system launch their enraged attacks, knowing well that if the prejudices are overthrown, the Kingdom of Man will have carried off one of its greatest victories.

Have these attacks attained their objectives? The response is both yes and no. They have succeeded in that they have conferred on the word prejudice a nuance of moral backwardness. Likewise, in a remarkably short time they have won to their ideas and to their cause vast sections of the young after-the-war generation. They have also been able, in an appreciable measure, to hoist their incoherent lucubrations to the level of an official philosophy and thereby to penetrate into the domain of education.

From the other side, the "anti-authoritarian" prophets have not succeeded except in the negative part of their design; they have simply destroyed. Their efforts aimed at creating a new man—free, harmonious, tolerant, and responsible—have not only miscarried, they have been counterproductive. Youth, which had been particularly solicited on the basis of their reformist zeal for a better world, give signs which directly contradict that which had been held up as the objective. Nervous disturbances, psychological upsets, intolerance and blind submission to political prophets and to ideological systems opposed to liberty are some of the current expressions, which are closely bound up with the practical realization of the "anti-authoritarian" programs. No one can contest it, but very few dare recognize it. It is a work of destruction accomplished in an astonishingly short time, and which cannot point to a single positive aspect.

Certainly there exist varieties of prejudice which can be utilized in the service of egotism and which can do great wrong to men. They can mask religious hypocrisy and bigotry. It happens that they serve private and family interests. Prejudice, finally, can degenerate into paranoid conceptions aimed at all which is foreign, in blind racial hatred, and in popular aggressiveness. One can abuse all that is human, and some will not fail to do so. This is part of our imperfect nature, and it is important not only to recognize it openly, but to bring into relief what is legitimate use and what is abuse, precisely in order to fight against the abuses. Its morbid manifestations must not lead one to consider that prejudice as such could be detrimental to humanity.

Prejudice is one of the great defensive arms of all human and social life. It aids us in the protection of all that is sacred, that which must not be soiled, that which we have the duty of defending and preserving in the work of God. It safeguards the psychic and physical health of the individual and of the family as well as their integrity; it assures the perpetuation of human communities; it remains as a force of conservation and as a guardian against the menace of corruption and disintegration.

Chapter 8
THE VEIL OF MAYA

If truth and falsehood were things that, to our sight as earthly beings, are clearly and distinctly distinguished the one from the other, our search for the truth would be much easier than it is in reality. If Satan manifests himself—literally or figuratively—with horns and cloven hooves, it would be much easier to discern the difference between good and evil, the true and the false. But in our world it is rare to meet truth and falsehood, good and evil, as things univocally defined and clearly differentiated. Much more frequently, one sees them mixed and in these *mélanges* it is certainly not a simple task to separate the good grain from the tares. Our world is not an elementary experience; it is full of contradictions and imperfections, of conflicts and oppositions. The truth, when it is presented to us, is neither simple, nor clear, nor seizable. In this baffling disorder, the words of St. Paul assume their full meaning: "In our earthly life, we do not see the truth clearly, but as in a mirror: we do not see it integrally, but fragmentarily."

Truth and falsehood, good and evil are not only intermixed in our eyes. They are also veiled. The divine creation is a flux that branches out even into the world of matter. It is a manifestation of omnipotence, and in this perspective the creature and his Creator are one. At the same time the manifested is separated from its divine origin in the same manner that an object is separated from its subject. God, as Creator, separates and objectifies his work by throwing—symbolically speaking— a veil over the creation. This is what the Vedanta calls "the veil of Maya."

This "veil of Maya" makes creation appear to us as separated from its Creator. At the same time it is He who permits us to experience the created as a reflection of the Creator. It is a question here of the duality of creation under its most elevated form: the created work is one with its Creator at the same time that it is separated from Him. This truth is not accessible to our reason. We are faced here with what one rightly calls the mystery of creation. Our existence is not veiled in this sense, that God would lead us astray and deliver us to the powers of delusion. The "veil of Maya" has for its primary objective to manifest this fundamental truth of all religion, namely, that God is the real and that the world, the veiled, is an illusion.*

To say that "life is a dream" is not a formula devoid of meaning. The reality which we seek must literally puncture the veil with which the Creator has covered his work, and it is our intellective faculty which makes this possible. If it was otherwise, the serpent of Paradise would have spoken truthfully; we could all eat of the tree of knowledge and become "like the gods." Terrestrial reality is not absolute, but relative and therefore imperfect; it is not eternal, but subordinate to the law of all that is transitory. It is an episode, a limited manifestation in time and space. Such is the signification of the "veil of Maya."

In a manner at once literal and figurative, humans find themselves "under" this veil and our terrestrial means do not permit us to elevate ourselves to a degree of knowledge implying the rending of the veil. But this knowledge of our limitation may also be

---

*The word *illusion*, though commonly used to translate *Maya*, should not be understood in the common acceptance of a mere figment of the imagination, as having no basis in reality. Rather should it be referred to the now seldom used *illude* which has the sense, among others, of: to play with, make sport of, mock, deceive with unfounded hopes, and so forth. Also implied is the notion of degrees of reality. —Translator's note.

deviated and false. This is what happens, for example, with deism. When the intellective light weakens, the theoreticians of deism turn up and declare that God no longer participates in his work. The deist error consists in regarding the "veil of Maya" as an impenetrable curtain behind which the Creator has retired. We see the work, say the deists, but we are not conscious of the author.

Appearances may lend some supporting evidence to the deists, because the more secularization and materialization are accentuated, the thicker grows the "veil of Maya" that is cast by the Creator over his work, at least from our earthly point of view. One comes to consider it as an impenetrable partition behind which is hidden the unknown author of the work. The divine presence and divine interventions become ever more difficult to grasp and finally men ask themselves if it is not the created that is real and the Creator an illusion. Then comes the time of satanic and total negation.

The veil which God has thrown over his creation and of which an object is to teach men to distinguish that which is real from that which is illusory, this veil becomes for them, in a time of mounting secularization, a pretext and means of detaching themselves from the principal cause of their life and of installing themselves here below as if the world was real. It is then ever more easy to mingle good and evil, to amalgamate lies and truth in a magic potion of ever increasing refinement which is served to our world. Confusion grows and one soon comes to disguise, to travesty, and to camouflage anything whatsoever, making of all existence a satanic masquerade. In this carnival lies are presented in the attire of truth and the militants of iniquity take "white as snow" airs of innocence, exactly as the carnival festivals offer to the basest street hooligans the occasion to parade in the uniform of a field marshall, or for the worst blasphemer to vest himself in the robes of a cardinal.

There is an intermediary zone where all is hazy and indistinct, where it is more and more difficult to discern the truth from the lie, the preferred domain of the spiritual "renovators" who always find there a more vast and more propitious terrain for their unscrupulous exploitation of the values of the Spirit. It is there where so many praiseworthy energies and so many good intentions are lost, for the means of separation between the truth and lies are always lacking.

All the satanic intrigues aim initially at the confusion that results from doubt. These states of confusion permit the entry of luciferian forces which relativize all values. Thanks to this relativism, Lucifer, "destroyer of peoples" as the prophet Isaiah calls him, can accomplish his design, which is to incite revolt against all power and all superior authority. Luciferian action must not be confused with the satanic, but it prepares the way for satanism which is the final reversal of the rapports of power, the victory of the lie and of wickedness over truth and goodness.

We have envisaged the "veil of Maya" under two aspects: the veil with which the Creator has covered His work and thanks to which it is objectivized and reflected by the author-subject, and at the same time that which, in our perspective, makes it possible to be conscious that the divine is real and the terrestrial illusory. There is yet another aspect. God is the hidden, and the hidden is also found in the world. Omnipotence is present in terrestrial manifestation as the being of things, as an immanent holiness which cannot be veiled. That must not be confused with the "nature" that Rousseau elevated to the rank of particular divinity of things and in virtue of which man could "realize" himself. The sacred character of the created work is its innocence, in its primordial purity, which man cannot derogate with impunity. The intimate being of nature, its most profound "secret," is and remains veiled and inaccessible to human knowledge. The "veil of Maya" does not envelope only the macrocosm, creation in its totality, it also withholds something of the microcosm, the created work with its particularities.

To the holiness of the world pertains not only the most intimate being of things but also all that which, of a cultural or ritual character, symbolizes and manifests the spiritual level—the Ark of the Covenant of the Israelites, the Holy of Holies behind the veil of the Temple, the altar enclosure, sanctuary of peace in the earthly sense where no murder could be committed, all that was hidden and separated from the profane world. That which is holy is always covered with a veil and is able to protect itself from all profanation, by withdrawal, by discretion, and by solitude. Even one of the greatest deniers of our times, Nietzsche, understood this: *Alles was tief ist, liebt die Maske.**

While the process of secularization, of transformation, and of destruction tends to thicken the hazy cover opposed to the penetration of the divine light in the minds of men, luciferian forces, from their side, seek with ever greater ardor to remove all that which opposes a human "vision" of terrestrial matters. Celestial light must be changed into darkness, but for the latter another word of order resounds: "The light, it is that which we intend." In the name of the luciferian search for truth, all the ways of access to the "secrets of nature" must now be opened. Rip open the veils, orders Lucifer! The profane light must penetrate into every nook and corner. Nothing must be left in obscurity, for that might interfere with the triumphal march of humanity.

All the reliquaries must be broken open, for what do they contain if not old bones and unrecoverable values? All sacred Scriptures will be studied, scrutinized in the light of rational knowledge and submitted to historical and scientific interpretations. Rationalism is raised to the level of wisdom and the pious man is taxed with naivety. But what is a man, after all? A body which is an ingenious biological mechanism—when one refers solely to the circulation of the blood—as was triumphally proclaimed, following the discovery by William Harvey in 1628; a soul which is an equally ingenious combination of energies and mental functions endowed with enormous potentials for development with a view of bringing happiness and power to human beings. One gives oneself up to a feverish search for laws and systems which must guide individuals and societies towards the harmonious order to which one considers man predestined.

One knows that "religion is the opium of the people." One places on the dissection table not only the body of man, but also his soul. The last line of defense of the sacred on earth has been forced by Sigmund Freud. Psychoanalysis has signaled the break-through

---

*All that is deep loves the mask.

of psychic surgery. Thc human soul must be "opened" to the new "scientific vision." One is assured that mental health consists in directing the luciferian light to the depths of the "hidden recesses" of the soul and in the drawing out of materials which will then be treated rationally. What hides in these dark depths especially is the constraining neurosis which constitutes religion; especially where religious opinions are encountered under the form of neurotic survivals. They must be destroyed, Freud said.[26] Surely man possesses an immortal soul which can neither be analyzed nor verbalized in terms of psychological science, but this objection is thrust aside by saying that it is a question precisely, of one of the most important veils to be rent: religion, not only as illusion, but as foyer of neurosis.

One of the articles of faith of luciferism is the following: if you know, you will fear nothing. Therefore knowledge is not only power: it also brings us psychic security, and this is one of the fundamental messages of Lucifer to humanity. It is also one of his most mendacious messages. For rational knowledge is nothing other than a research without respite in the world of forms, and because of this the quest for this knowledge is a separative process: in his rational research, man becomes more and more isolated. The more he amasses of factual notions, the further he pushes the structural analysis of the world of sensible phenomena, and the more he understands how hopeless it is to find an interior psychic security in this way. He is relegated to his solitude, his separativity, his isolation, things which inevitably go hand in hand with the world of rationalism.

Religion is not a stifling neurosis and the elimination of the last religious opinions is not the equivalent of liberating humanity from its last neurotic vestiges. On the contrary, it is the

---

[26]Sigmund Freud, *Die Zukunft einer Illusion* [*The Future of an Illusion*], Gesammelte Werke 14 (London, 1948), pp. 367ff. The book ends with a profession of faith in science: "Nein, unserer Wissenschaft is keine Illusion. Eine Illusion aber ware es zu glauben, dass wir anderswoher bekommen konnten, was sie uns nicht geben kann" (ibid., p. 380). ["No, science is no illusion. But it would be an illusion to suppose that we could get anywhere else what it cannot give us."—ET, p. 102.]

secular world surrounding us which is stamped with a growing psychic insecurity; and if it is incapable of giving to men psychic security, it is an effect of growing rationalism. Instead of disappearing from the world illuminated by luciferian light, neuroses increase.

Luciferism has yet another argument to put forward and we must examine it. When we rend the veil under the pretext of elucidating reality, many things that are noxious, unclean, sickly, and perverse are discovered. Is that desirable? Yes, reply the militants of the luciferian avant-garde. For if, in exhibitionist dizziness, we strip to the buff that which is morbid and filthy, we shine the light on it, this salubrious illumination takes away from these obscenities all the power of seduction that they exercise when they remain hidden. This extreme but ever more widely accepted opinion is found especially in the subject of sexuality, so that one is here in the presence of a sort of inverse puritanism: the smut, it is declared, must "disappear in the sunlight."

With that, luciferism rapidly approaches the point of maturation where it will be incumbent upon satanism to resume the work on its own account. It is the time of the complete inversion or revolution. The lie is installed in the place of truth, wickedness in the place of goodness. The worldly obscuration has reached a degree at which the luciferian pseudo-light is received as a consolation and a direction even in the situations where its noxiousness must be evident to all. It is declared that the state of sickness and of perversion is the equivalent of the normal, and then all notion of a norm is questioned. One cannot come closer to chaos.

We must recall once more the words of Baudelaire: "The cleverest of the ruses of the devil is to persuade us that he does not exist." The partisans of *aggiornamento* should reflect on this. Incessant secularization has created an intermediary zone of misrepresentation, of masquerade, of mixture of good and evil, of the true and the false; we come to grips with all this under the most subtle and the most attractive forms. It is surely not always easy to discern evil, and the luciferian forces have an easy task when they want to legitimize and support their action. Lucifer is always able to count on the willing cooperation of fellow travelers for aid and support. Among these there are numerous supporters of religion. It comes about that they discover—unfortunately, too late in many cases—that it would have been better to refuse such collaboration. For the objective is not always announced with as much clarity as Sigmund Freud showed when he chose to place in exergue in his *The Interpretation of Dreams*, the Latin epigram: *Flectere si nequeo superos, Acheronta movebo* (If I cannot bend the gods, I will stir up Hell).*

---

*Virgil, *Aeneid*, 7.312.

Chapter 9
TOLERANCE

"Be ye therefore perfect as your Father in heaven is perfect." This saying of Christ may seem baffling. It is, in that it seems to pose an absolute requirement in an order marked by relativity and imperfection. How is this to be explained? Is it not unreasonable to demand that the perfect should be realized on the level of the imperfect?

The command of Christ is not a moral exhortation. Morality is tied to our existential life. It must therefore be manifested, which it is under the form of laws and precepts. The just and the unjust, in the earthly sense, take a normative bearing valid for relations between humans, having our imperfect world for field of application. In commanding us to be perfect as our heavenly Father is perfect, Christ cannot therefore be addressing a moral injunction to us, nor can he be furnishing us a rule of conduct. It is an exhortation aiming at imitation and which concerns the order of the virtues.

Morality is a terrestrial affair; virtue, on the other hand, is the encounter between divine perfection and human life insofar as this encounter is the ideal attitude. Morality concerns the world and therefore consists in a horizontal relationship. Virtue is a relationship with God and is thus a vertical relationship. The words of Christ designate an imitation, an aspiration which must not be situated in this world with its contradictions and its moral rules. It is related to an effort towards the interior, towards the spiritual center. This is why the exhortation to perfection is not unreasonable, but on the contrary admits of a necessity; it indicates the search for the Me that every human being carries within himself as a parcel of spiritual perfection.[27]

It is a question therefore of an injunction aimed at the interior and not the exterior; it is not a question of our earthly and profane life. The Sermon on the Mount, of which it is a part, is itself a hymn of praise to virtue, an exhortation to imitation, and this is the message which is addressed to us as creatures destined for eternity. Thence the apparently irrational injunctions that Jesus enunciates in the Sermon on the Mount receive their true sense. He, Himself, who had seized the whip to chase the merchants from the Temple, did not formulate any pacifist precept when He exhorted us to turn the other cheek to an earthly aggressor, any more than He dreamed of favoring delinquency when He recommended, not only to let the thief take one's tunic, but to give him also one's cloak. There is nothing in the Sermon on the Mount that urges the distribution of terrestrial goods, any more than economic irresponsibility, but it is an exhortation to give priority to the spiritual before the temporal, to submit oneself totally to the will of the heavenly Father, so that no power here below, especially not Mammon, can contest the place which is due Him: "No one can serve two masters." Nor must it be deduced that we should not have the right to bring judgments in earthly matters. The precept "judge not" signifies that we have neither the power nor the right to anticipate the judgments of the Last Day by condemnations, acquittals, or prescriptions.

The Sermon on the Mount is an inestimable esoteric document, a hymn to virtue, an injunction to seek the truth and the interior life and not the life of the world where the worms and the moths destroy. Nothing could be more false than to interpret it as an ethical document or as a program of social morality. It relates to that which is holy, not to that which is ephemeral, and it requires of

---

[27]The author has treated the relationships between virtue and morality in a previous work, *Mellan Himmel och Jord* [*Between Heaven and Earth*] (Stockholm, 1970), pp. 39ff.

man only this: to imitate—it being understood that this imitation is an interior attitude and not social behavior. The tree which bears good fruit does not procure a terrestrial nourishment. It is spiritual fruits which virtue places in reserve. Similarly with bad fruits, the tree that bears them must be destroyed because these fruits bring ruin.

Thus the Sermon on the Mount issues into an absolute exigency, an imperative of virtue, if you will: "Every good tree bears good fruit, but an evil tree bears evil fruit." That does not permit any exceptions. It is like two roads which diverge. The way of virtue is absolute in that it leads to a spiritual reality bearing the signature of perfection. The way of morality is an effort to maintain, in a limited sphere and in the measure of human strength, an absolute in a world that is relative, contradictory, and imperfect. Morality brings a superior message to the inferior level of the earth; it is a descent of the truth and of virtue into this fragmentary and incomplete world. Morality is subordinate to virtue and it is only from this latter that it draws its persuasive force, while morality itself as well as the rules that it controls is fragmentary, contradictory and imperfect.

Every tree that does not bear good fruit will be cut down and thrown into the fire. Such is the message of the Sermon on the Mount. It concerns virtue. But how must we understand it here below, in the world of morality? No man, no regime on this earth is without fault. One cannot certify that any tree here below will always produce good fruit. All bear the mark of imperfection, however sincere may be our intentions and our efforts. We cannot therefore blame ourselves, neither our social institutions. We cannot condemn terrestrial imperfection, for it is an existential fact impossible to eliminate. What we can do, in compensation, and which we have the duty to do, is to examine the sources of our terrestrial nourishment. This is not a question of condemning the imperfection here below, but rather the doctrines and the currents which inspire us. It behooves us once again to meditate on the words of the Sermon on the Mount: "Beware of false prophets, for they will come to you in sheep's clothing."

In direct contrast, the Kingdom of Man comes to us saying: make of the human soul a *tabula rasa*, a clean slate, and let us search without, in the exterior, for a knowledge of existence. This counsel has already been given by Francis Bacon. In this world each step that we take is a step into the unknown. The true and the false, the just and the unjust are notions, so it is pretended, of which we have no direct preexistent knowledge. It is only after the fact, under the effect of a constant process of "trial and error," that something takes shape which, temporarily at least, may have some value as criterion of the true and the just. Justice which, vertically, is the equilibrium between the will of God and that of man; and, horizontally, that which rules the cosmic order, must be converted into an "equilibrium" attainable only by empirical means and which in reality is only a provisional state with a constantly changing content.

This astonishing comedy cannot be played without observing certain fundamental rules. Because man is regarded as a *tabula rasa* and each decision necessarily having been submitted to the "trial and error" process beforehand, it is necessary that an entire liberty of thought and action reign. One must, therefore, challenge all orthodoxy and all attachment to absolute truths and immutable values. But, in order that this spectacle of a humanity entirely free in its thought and acts may endure, an essential rule is necessary: tolerance. For in this swarming mass of life, of ideas and activities, the most divergent and the most controversial things must likewise have their possibility of expression.

Tolerance is a notion that intervenes at the beginning of the process of secularization under the form of polemical negation of ecclesiastical and princely absolutism. To be tolerant in this initial sense assuredly does not represent a particularly compromising attitude. "Crush the infamy," cried Voltaire, naming thus the Church of Christ. What he wanted, he and those on his side, was to pass off this call, doubled with unsparing attacks on all orthodoxy and all religious ritualism, for an expression of tolerance.

The situation differs totally when the "infamy" has been crushed. Tolerance as protest against a real or supposed privation of liberty is one thing; tolerance in the face of all sorts of antagonistic demonstrations in a situation of liberty is something else. In the first case it is a question of undoing norms and doctrinaire systems. The objective is then as simple as it is close at hand: it is total heterodoxy. In the second case one finds oneself in an entirely new situation. When the walls of temples have been denuded and the sacred objects have been thrown into the dung heap or stacked in the cellars of museums, when every norm and every principle are considered as provisional, then the children of the Kingdom of Man are charged with a burden under which they may truly stumble. How can men who think only of their own interests, full of pride and of egotism, encouraged to seize their part of the "banquet of life"—how can they observe between themselves relationships of generosity while so many divergent opinions, desires, and motives for action clash with one another?

This leads us to the second tendency included under this same rubric. The relativism of values creates a provisional state which is a field of battle where each one would have the right to express freely his thoughts and his desires. The hostilities conducted in the name of tolerance take the form of debate. This latter presupposes that a preexistent truth does not exist, but that the "true" and the "best" would be comparable to fragments that one could assemble, thanks to the shock of ideas produced in free discussion. That supposes in its turn that all participants in the debates are animated by a common will, that of uniting their efforts in view of reaching that which they positively believe can be considered a noble end result of the debate—the truth. How this precious fruit can ripen among the internecine struggles to which egotisms and special interests give themselves, this is an issue on which, even in the interior of the system, doubt seems to prevail.

No reasonable creature questions the value of the exchange of ideas. But in order to assure the liberty of these exchanges, two conditions must be fulfilled: that those who think differently should benefit from a true tolerance and that the exchange concern essential subjects and lead to durable results. Not one of these conditions prevail in the Kingdom of Man. Debate is a means of struggle in the hands of egoist forces who work for themselves and who treat tolerance as a luxury that is useless for their interests. Any deepening of the discussion is carefully avoided. For one would see with overmuch evidence, if the interlocutors should there encounter eternal truths, the fallacy of supposing that a debate or a dialogue could be a selective process permitting the reunion of scattered "fragments of truth." The discussion would immediately come to a stop.

This must not be allowed to happen. The anxiety with which the participants in these debates avoid every effort to deepen them shows one thing: a "therapeutic" role is attributed to these dialogues and discussions, a means of giving some tension to mental life, of dispelling ceaselessly menacing sadness, engaging men in a dialectical game devoid of any real aim. This "therapeutic" effect is sought in the vivacity of the debate of which the intensity grows in proportion as the objects under discussion are peripheral. One comes thus to the result aimed at: to hinder the actualization of eternal truths, and thereby, the establishment of inner tranquility.

The directors watch over this kaleidoscopic game. Long since, tolerance has lost its role of polemical negation of religious and monarchial absolutism. Today, that which one refers to by "tolerance" is a means of extirpating the last vestiges of a normative order anchored in the divine order itself. There is no longer any place in this secularized world for an authentic tolerance. For when egotistical man, subordinate to his sensory interests, has full scope to seek only his own advantage, the notion of tolerance loses its meaning. His neighbor then is changed into an obstacle in his way.

Is tolerance, therefore, a deceitful term? As long as we give it an exclusively profane sense, the question must be answered affirmatively. But if we see in it an expression of longanimity towards human imperfection, it receives its veritable content. Longanimity can be founded only on love for one's neighbor, and this love itself is a word without meaning if in its turn it is not founded on the love existing between the Creator and His creature. "To love one's neighbor" does not cease to be an empty formula until we effectively accept the same Father and when in consequence our neighbors are our brothers.

There are too many imperfections, too much ugliness in the world to be able to "love" all of our neighbors in the same manner in which we are fond of those who are most dear. But that of which we must remain conscious in spite of all that separates us, is that we have the same Father, which imposes on us the ties of human obligation which take concrete form in numerous ways. Negatively, we can say that all of us participate in existential imperfection, and positively, we can express this rapport in showing longanimity to our brothers, even while we hope from them a reciprocal attitude. Our imperfection is an existential "debt" that we all assume; we cannot, without regard for others, thrust from our own shoulders the part of the burden that is incumbent upon us and charge our brothers with it.

The essence of true tolerance is long-suffering. It is there that the incompatibility appears with what is called tolerance in the Kingdom of Man. Given that every person can "save himself in his own way," one can align oneself with no matter what opinion. But that is not tolerance. That is indifference, notably towards one's neighbor and his spiritual life. That is why the debates can attack all values and go so far as to violate that which is ascribable to true tolerance. If something is regarded as indifferent, that is as much as to say such things can be annihilated at any time by anybody. Then the champions of the system say that anyone can attack that which is holy as much as he wishes, for it is always permitted to declare to the defenders of the sacred that they are free, that they can defend themselves—which means "discuss" that which is holy—because they benefit from "religious liberty."

That which one calls tolerance then becomes its contrary. The debate becomes a legitimation of intolerance. For in the name of "liberty," we have the right in principle to attack, to outrage everyone and everything, for the one we attack enjoys the same right! Yet the true tolerance founded on long-suffering cannot be indifferent to my opinions nor to those of my neighbors. All of us participate in a transcendent truth which is rendered conscious in our hearts. In consequence, we try, we and our neighbors, to come to a comprehension of this truth that is as just and unanimous as possible. It is there that tolerance arises and where it is itself put to the test. We then become aware of tolerance in the form of longanimity, which must contain a quality that is totally foreign to the Kingdom of Man: patience.

We must be ever ready to meet a divergence, a false doctrine, just as we must be ever ready to find ourselves accused of deviating from the way of truth. Our longanimity and patience must be proven ceaselessly. We cannot simply "crush the infamous thing" which allows an opinion different from that which we regard as just. Wars of religion and theological struggles seem cruelly to give the lie to all that one can say of longanimity and patience, but one must not forget that it is often a question of manifestations of the divine Word differing in time and space, confrontations which cannot lead to immediate ecumenical fraternizations. If we infringe the principles of tolerance, if our human imperfection arouses conflicts where peace should reign, one cannot find there arguments against tolerance as an ideal of virtue for our common terrestrial existence.

It seems at first glance that a strict orthodoxy is always a system privative of spiritual liberty, and it is against this orthodoxy that, for centuries, the apostles of profane tolerance have directed their assults. Assuredly it is necessary that those in power in an orthodox order keep themselves from all oppression and from all excess. That would be abuse of power and profound injustice; furthermore, the immutable doctrine of the divine truth must be an aid and a protection for everyone, in such a manner that in his terrestrial life man may develop his personal particularities in security.

In the modern system, on the other hand, where humanity is proclaimed the real divinity with, for attributes, the "immortal rights of man," it follows that these billions of "divine" and sovereign beings must be made as homogeneous and "equal" as possible. The result comes quickly. It is an apparent paradox—but one in fact conforming to an internal logic—that one sees in ancient orthodox and authoritarian societies greater diversity and variety marking the terrestrial life of men, while our secularized world with all its liberty and all its debates, on the contrary witnesses to a growing conformism. In the modern mass democracies there exists an attitude of ostracism which certainly does not correspond to the liberal promises announcing the advent of a free and tolerant humanity.

The Kingdom of Man is at an impasse. Even profane tolerance is revealed as illusory. The sentiment spreads that the promised happiness, liberty, and tolerance must be sought elsewhere. Will the prophets of the system sound retreat? Will one make the formidable self-criticism consisting in the recognition that all was false, that the ways leading to human happiness were not practicable? Will one tell the men who have gone astray and are confused to return to the sources of truth?

The prophets are not yet anywhere near ready to lay down their arms. For an issue will always exist: the grand liquidation, the spectacular act of purification in which all the ancient must be reduced to dust in order that a new world and a new man might be reborn from the cinders, as promised. A fire will destroy, will purify, will renew: the revolution.

Chapter 10
REVOLUTION

There have always been found, on the occasion of the internal hostilities of humanity, individuals who have wanted to raise themselves up to a position of tyrannical power, or who have used and abused tyrannically power with which they have been invested or which they have inherited. Do we have the right to rise against them, to thrust them aside, even to kill them? These questions have been the object of passionate discussions, particularly in the Middle Ages. The murder of the tyrant is not only a political problem, but it is especially one of a moral and religious character.

David is ceaselessly menaced by Saul. But when the opportunity is offered to rid himself of his enemy, he does not take advantage of it. There was the case of the grotto serving as a refuge for him and his companions, which the king entered alone; the same as when David found him sleeping soundly with his men. For David said, "The Lord be merciful unto me that I extend not my hand upon the Lord's anointed!"[28] In fact, if the tyrant is a veritable sovereign, a monarch designated and established by God, he cannot be killed.

But can we refuse obedience to the tyrant, and in what manner? According to a common opinion, we have the right to

---

[28] 1 Samuel, 24, 26.

refuse to obey a tyrant, to hide ourselves, and to flee in order to avoid the application of or submission to laws and ordinances decreed by a tyrannical prince in contradiction to the laws of God and of nature. But kill him? Never.

Such also is the advice of Martin Luther. And even an innovative thinker as radical as Jean Bodin, the greatest political philosopher of the sixteenth century, was of this opinion. Despite all the evil that he may commit, we do not have the right to kill the tyrant. Bodin establishes a parallel with the relations between father and son; even if the father murders and commits all sorts of evil acts, even if he merits the most rigorous punishments, his son does not have the right to kill him. It is the same in the case of the prince, Bodin believes: the former has been designated by God and cannot therefore be killed by the hand of man.[29]

To kill a terrestrial sovereign who is anointed by the Lord is therefore equivalent to parricide. That comes down to attacking something that has been instituted by God. It is different with the right of resistance. The Christian Middle Ages had lively discussions on this subject. One can envisage many ways in which one would have the right, and even the duty of resisting a government which might strike at divine and earthly law. The possibility always exists of retiring passively and fleeing, but more militant means must not be excluded. A general upheaval is a violent revolt against an oppression with the objective of a true change of regime. Revolt has a more limited aim: to change the custodian of power, individual or collective, without seeking to modify profoundly the order of things. But the general upheaval, like revolt, can be accomplished in the cadre of a divine as well as a terrestrial order, and their final objective may be precisely the reestablishment of such an order as had been upset. Revolution, on the contrary, is essentially different.

Revolution is the total elimination of an existing order and the installation of a new order. New values, new criteria, new articles of faith, new systems and structures must be established. Revolution is not only, like general upheaval, a violent insurrection against an

---

[29]Jean Bodin, *The Six Books of the Republic* (Lyon, 1593), pp. 297ff. and 306ff.

oppression in view of forming a new regime. Nor is it, like revolt, an action undertaken to put an end to a power deemed intolerable. Revolt and general upheaval can be part—and often are—of preliminaries leading to or pertaining to a revolutionary process. But it is only with revolution itself that a total reversal is produced: the plus and minus signs are inverted. This reversal can take place on the social and economic level; it can be of a philosophical, political, or cultural character. Most often it intervenes in all these domains. In fact, hardly any sector of human life escapes; for in its essence it is universal and concerns principles as well as humanity in its ensemble.

Upheaval and revolt seek to abolish abuses and disequilibria limited in time and space. They do not grasp any principle of the established order, seeking on the contrary to respect principles in their pure and original state. Upheaval and revolt demand reestablishment. Revolution, on the contrary, aims at the annihilation of an order. It aims at the heights. It attacks authority itself; it is, in its essence, anti-authoritarian. It is in this sense that its principles are received. Its keynotes, its agitation, may be addressed to a national entity, to ethnic or social groups, but they always carry a message that concerns all men. In this respect, the revolution has value for the totality of the human race. It knows no limit, neither in time nor in space; it is universal. It has the pretention to announce an "eternal" truth.

The order to which the Creator has subjected us knows no revolution and no upset susceptible of making created things submit to any change of principle. Men have only this choice: to obey or disobey. This is the alternative before which the Creator has placed us. Consequently revolution is an attack against all created hierarchy as well as a refusal of celestial paternity which, in its ultimate limits, ends—symbolically speaking—in collective parricide, because revolution rejects the obedience which we owe to our Creator. Such is the inevitable consequence of its universal pretentions.

The seizure of power by the Kingdom of Man thus takes place on the highest level of manifestation. Revolution is the most implacable of all human actions. It destroys the bridges and puts fire to the churches. It exalts and glorifies illegitimacy. Every revolutionary act is a collective work that does not leave any place to any deviation whatsoever which might satisfy the desires or needs of individuals. For the revolution is not made for individuals, but for that figure of mystical legend that is called Man, and of which the collective manifestation is called the People. It is Man, it is the People that must be liberated, purified, reborn.

Revolution is the inverse of Paradise in the sense that man must be purified of all that has corrupted him. In this total inversion, the satanic character of revolution appears: a new man must arise from the revolutionary process. The great symbol which will dominate the others will therefore be fire. For, in the hands of revolutionaries, torches will not have as their primary role the giving of light. The flaming torches will light great bonfires. There is a double role for fire: to burn and consume the ancient, and at the same time to purge and to make healthy. Fire melts metal and the pure gold is separated from the dross. Each revolution is a secular purgatory.

Every revolutionary movement has a favorable debut. It can denounce and join battle with abuses that are so crying and so obvious that they incur the sharpest condemnations quite beyond revolutionary circles. These latter, consciously or not, always utilize notions of "paradise" or original innocence and of the fall. But the restoration of the "paradisiacal" state does not imply a return to the sources of creation. This point marks an essential difference: the revolution is a "development." When men will have accomplished their revolution, it is pretended, they will recover themselves on a different and higher level; the revolution therefore will be a step in the supposed march of humanity towards a higher form of perfection.

From an historical point of view, there exist in our epoch two revolutionary stages. The great French Revolution of 1789 proclaimed the advent of man, universal and all powerful. He no longer takes into consideration the warning of the Creator on the subject of the tree of knowledge. He will be atomically free, manifesting only himself, and simultaneously he will be a generous citizen and above particular interests: enormous contradiction, for no one can be at the same time interested and disinterested. All the ties which, spatially, have united men to families, to tribes, to nations, to peoples, as well as all those which, temporally, attach them to lines of tradition or which tie generations together, must be cut. The new divinity of the earth has been proclaimed: it is Man.

The other stage is the revolution of 1917. Just as the great French Revolution had been preceded by a long period of preparation and must be considered as the culminating point of a long revolutionary process, the Bolshevik Revolution of 1917 in Russia is the political outcome of a doctrine which is distinguished from the ideas of 1789 as sharply as East from West. Man who, in the Declaration of his rights as in the intellectual world of the Jacobin Club, introduces himself as above the world of matter and as dominating it, finds himself in the Marxist order entirely included in this material world. The human mind is nothing other than a reflection of that which comes to pass in the material substance of the world (*das Ideelle ist das im Menschenkopf umgesetzte Materielle*).* Existence has only one dimension, which is material, and it is deployed only on the horizontal level constituted by the earth on which man lives. Enclosed in his own sensory materiality, man cannot live otherwise than as a social being. *Der vergesellschaftete Mensch*** is a creature who is nothing other than a support for the process of production and of reproduction conditioned by a material base.

The secular dream of the Kingdom of Man, which is the limitless empire of the earth, attains its apogee with the Marxist-communist revolutions. Man, thinks the Marxist, has now resolved once and for all his problems of identity; he has been liberated from all degrading slavery, is free in the Hegelian sense, and with the communist society, effects the "leap into the kingdom of liberty." Capitalism, that "last antagonistic form" of the development of

*The ideal is the material transposed in the human brain.

**Man in the social state.

human society, where the proletarian is an incomplete creature, pressured and alienated both insofar as producer and as man, has been cast down and annihilated. It is only in the final communist phase where the fundamental rule prevails: "from each according to his capacity, to each according to his needs," that man will have found himself again with his identity. Such is the communist postulate.

The Marxist conception of reality issued from the theories of the last century on a material world defined and determined by immutable natural laws. This is why the Marxist believes that he is supported by solid ground. He believes he can place man in a fixed temporal and spatial order: in time and in space, "Soviet man" imperturbably follows his route towards the "realization of himself." In time, elevated to History according to the true Hegelian spirit, the achievement implying the resolution of human conflicts is dialectically produced. In space, that is to say, in the second of the two pseudo-divinities of Marxism—Matter—man and society fashion themselves into a synthesis, or in Marxist language, into a dialectical unity, marking the end of all internal human and social struggles.

There is in communism a very important tendency, one to which inadequate attention is generally given: that which would reestablish the social order, the cosmos, which liberal society was in the process of destroying in the nineteenth century. Liberal heterodoxy must be replaced therefore with Marxist orthodoxy. Liberal relativism, lacking tradition, and superficial cosmopolitanism must give place to an order in which the individual and society will constitute a dialectical unity. The Bolshevik regimes have enclosed their "Soviet men" in an orthodox system dependent on time and space as these notions were held to be true in the last century.

Temporally, this "Soviet man" is tied to a Hegelian-Marxist conception of history which is the orthodox doctrine of dialectical development to which humanity is subject. Spatially, it depends on the material world, and thanks also to the cold war and to the greatly encouraged Soviet patriotism, it has been maintained in a national identity which has contributed conspicuously to the protection of its Marxist faith from contamination. This orthodoxy has been able to subsist in a closed state system where the party with its apparatus, its politburo and its ideologies has been relatively successful in preserving its credo from contagion. Thus the "Soviet man" has been educated in a tradition solidly rooted in time and space. Thus it has been possible for it to preserve a consciousness of identity, with temporal and spatial dimensions, presenting a clearly conservative character.

A paradoxical situation has resulted from this in that the communist, "popular democratic" regimes bear a strong impress of traditionalism and conservatism, which may be verified on the social and individual levels as well as in such domains as those of pedagogy and aesthetics. Is it a question of a definitive state? The Marxist believes that the communist revolution is the last one in the historical evolution of humanity, for it implies the elimination of the bourgeois and capitalist orders which represent the "last antagonistic form" of the social life of men. With communism, man is declared freed from his degrading slavery; as a productive being, he lives in harmony with his work since he is supposedly no longer the object of any exploitation. He is also considered as living in profound harmony with society, since the suppression of social classes is considered to make man and society a "dialectical unity." Man is then promised a development without conflicts in the direction of his material and spiritual perfection. For one of the fundamental postulates of Marxist thought is psychological determinism which finds here its expression in the idea that the unlimited needs of men keep pace with the equally unlimited and incessant efforts to satisfy them.

According to Marxism, the history of humanity is thus ended, it being given that dialectically, it reaches a final synthesis, all that being in accordance with Hegelian views. The world of matter, therefore, would attain a perfection finding its expression in the development, ever more pronounced, of the sensory and psychic aspect of this material world. This is why Marxist "humanism" defines itself ever more precisely: it is a question of the ultimate man. Following profane and classical humanistic conceptions, communism considers man as a substantial, indestructible unity. Thus Karl Marx could say: *Das hochste Wesen fur den Mensch ist der Mensch selbst.**

That which Marxism does not see, or refuses to see, is that it methodically destroys the very base of its own work. Totally secularized sensory man, one with the material world, is then in reality only a part of this sensory world over which he is supposed to reign. But how can the part reign over the whole? It is literally immersed in matter and finds itself in the same situation as he who, plunged in mid-ocean, would think himself able to withdraw himself without aid.

But there is more. In his negation of all spirituality, Marxist man comes to the point that he loses even the consciousness of his "me." For, despite centuries of profane humanistic preaching, this latter leads to the loss of the consciousness of one's self, because it separates itself from the source of self-consciousness which is our immortal soul. Like Western capitalism, the communist system can produce well ordered mechanics, workers functioning as perfectly as ants, and creatures abandoned to vegetative leisure. The inevitable consequence of such a system is a man who in the end comes to be nothing but a sum of functional fragments which, in a mechanical fashion, receives information, works it over, and transmits it further on. It is there that the East and the West meet in a startling fashion. On this point there is no difference of principle between the capitalist and communist worlds, for both rest on a secularized philosophy, the false doctrine of egalitarian and sovereign Man. Certainly the capitalist world professes a bourgeois-liberal liberty while communist regimes pretend to a social liberation from capitalist exploitation. The error is the same on the one side and on the other. In totally secularized sensory existence, the consciousness of the "me" ends sooner or later in its ruin.

The East and the West have both sought to the very end to cling to the determinist conception inherited from the last centuries which represents existence as a coherent order, obeying laws,

---

*For man, the supreme Being is man himself.

where man, thanks to his superior mental faculties, can move forward and give himself to all sorts of beautiful experiments for the amelioration of the world. The rapid development of the natural sciences in the course of this century has completely destroyed this image of the world. There no longer exists a solid material base, there are no longer eternal and immutable natural laws, and human knowledge does not suffice to embrace a true and complete image of reality. The absolute is no longer found in the sensory world. This absolute must be sought elsewhere by the inhabitants of the Kingdom of Man; this is what men of wisdom and piety have known for thousands of years.

In this regard there is no difference of principle between East and West. Whether one is a subject of the capitalist or communist world, one is sunk in "popular sovereignty," egalitarian and orphaned, in the sensory sector of existence, in the relativist current of matter, or, according to Norbert Weiner, principal philosophical interpreter of this new situation, in the sea of entropy. The only means of saving oneself from this drowning is then to transform oneself into a technical organ which, Weiner thinks, one can do thanks to the "islets" to which one clings in order to continue to live as a biological being. Man must consider himself a machine, he thinks, for this would be the only possibility of salvation. There would be a great similarity between the nervous system and an automatic machine in that the one and the other take their decisions on the base of other decisions taken in the past. This biological machine that constitutes man is in principle therefore nothing but a computer.[30]

Viewed superficially, the revolutionary movements, socialist, communist, anarchist, seem on the way to achieving definitively and globally the revolutionary work commenced in 1917. All over

---

[30]"From the perspective of the computer, the individuality of the soul resides in what it preserves of precedent instructions and memories, which it develops along ways already established. Just as a computer can be utilized as a model for the construction of other computers, one can imagine that a living individual divides himself into two individuals sharing the same past but developing ever more divergently. This is what happens with twins issuing from a single egg, but there is no reason why the same thing cannot happen

the world young revolutionaries erect barricades, uttering their curses against "authoritarian structures" and promising to replace them with a "living democracy." In reality, it is a new revolution that is under way, but it is silent and without barricades. It is the inevitable revolution logically following the two preceding.

The French Revolution had proclaimed the advent of profane man, of the autonomous individual, all-powerful citizens of the Kingdom of Man. The Russian Revolution pursued the destructive work in making this individual an integral part of all-powerful matter, with a soul that is nothing other than a projection of this material world. The third revolution, silent and without barricades, is the logical development of the two that preceded, principally in that it manifests and achieves the destruction of itself contained in all the anterior revolutionary tendencies. Secularized man loses his identity, in materialism, even to the possibility of maintaining the illusion of a spirituality, as he was still able to do in humanistic "spirituality." It is an interior disintegration, a process of decomposition going on without arrest. No one chronicles this revolution. There are no public manifestations, no cliché posters, no distribution of programs. This is why we say of this revolution that it is silent and without barricades.

In our epoch, when the young combatants of the barricades brandish their red and black flags while swearing to reduce all to cinders in order to erect on the ruins a more just world, this must not be confounded with the revolution that we have in view. For this latter, which is interior, reveals itself constantly on the exterior by acts of violence. Vacuity, absurdity, absence of identity and of paternity, despair, manifest themselves in fits of fury against "authoritarian structures" and "established interests." These riots and barricades do not make a revolution by themselves; they are acts of revolt and upheaval which must not dissimulate the true revolutionary process which goes on under the form of an interior and personal disintegration.

---

with what one calls the soul and that without a simultaneous division of the body." Norbert Weiner, *Materia, Maskiner, Maniskor* (Stockholm, 1964), p. 115.

This absence of identity, of consciousness of one's "me" and of paternity is accompanied by an ever more marked absence of maturity, and a result of this is an incapacity to assume human relationships in a normal and adult fashion. Such a condition, characterized by a lowered maturity and by a growing confusion, leaves no other possibility to the new generations but to seek on an inferior level the satisfaction of their needs for a common life. As there is no paternity and hence no fraternity—the one is the condition of the other—"symbiotic" coexistence is reduced to a state characterized by nihilism and chaos.

In this "symbiotic" and infantile manner of living together, there exists neither comradeship nor true solidarity, but only the solitude of the creature devoted to himself. At the same time there is no more demarcation. For symbiosis involves the elimination of a sentiment lived during each process of maturation, which is the consciousness of the "me" and the "thee," of the rapport between the adult and the adolescent, between the strong and the weak, and similarly for sex, for love, for mercy, and for responsibility.

It is from this "symbiotic" confusion that the revolution presently looms. It is not a revolt under the sign of strength, but of weakness. A young man, healthy and virile, lives in a state of vital tension with his father, for he wants to become a father himself one day. The image of the father is constantly before his eyes. On the other hand, the "symbiotic" rebel, in the weakness of his person and in his lack of maturity, lances desperate attacks against every father image, because he would destroy it. And if he would destroy the image it is because he does not desire to and could not become a fully mature father. It is in such states of childish backwardness and debility that the "anti-authoritarian" tendencies of our time prosper.

Then all limits are obliterated from consciousness. Like the slogan, we must live in a "world without frontiers," it must be forgotten that all creation is a formal and limited world in which, as human beings, we must know not only that frontiers exist but also where they are drawn: frontiers between man and woman, between child and adult, between the beautiful and the ugly, between good and evil, between truth and falsehood. The "absence of frontiers" in space must also be applied to time. The bridges must be destroyed, before and behind. This silent revolution produces a man "without history," for whom the past appears indifferent and every action seems equally indifferent in relation to its effects in the future. Time becomes a stunted "now," while space is considered "without end." Both thenceforth seem indifferent. This permits the new revolution to remove the supports of two keystones of human existence: the conceptions of time and space are in the way of disappearing from the consciousness of man.

Robespierre and Lenin both had the firm conviction of having definitively delivered humanity. They were mistaken. There is yet a revolution to make, and it is precisely the one which is underway. This third revolution is only the harvest which ripens from the seed of the preceding two. It is a revolution in the void, confusion and the loss of identity. The proud vessel of the Kingdom of Man inexorably founders in the chaos under preparation for centuries by man himself. When God is not there, anything can happen, Dostoyevsky tells us, and this is the bitter discovery made by the coryphaei of the system.

In order that man can fulfill his mission on earth, or only in order that his life here may be supportable, order is necessary, interiorly and exteriorly. Interior order proceeds from the consciousness that man has an immortal soul and that he is thereby united to his Creator. It is this which gives him a consciousness of identity, a personality in the metaphysical as well as in the terrestrial sense.

The exterior order flows from this interior consciousness. Man knows his limits; he knows that he must live his short life on earth in the cadre of the limits of time and space. In the course of this existence he is in the grip of constant difficulties which each one must surmount in the measure of his capacity. And that he may have to resort to violence sometimes, we know only too well. We are not ignorant, either, that ancient regimes have been swept away and replaced by others. These are facts. But this must not be confused with the revolution. This latter leads to chaos because it is, in its essence, the antipodes of the divine, that is, it is satanism. In the face of the divine order, satanic chaos raises itself up. Chaos comes to birth in the heart of men as a rupture of equilibrium which follows upon the forgetfulness of the truth which all carry within themselves. That, we must always remember.

Chapter 11
LOVE

Secularization is a fish in troubled waters. It in no way signifies, as its spokesmen like to suggest, that men would turn aside from religious "superstition" in order to find light and perspicuity in rationalism. Secularization, on the contrary, implies the loss by man of his capacity of objectivation, of his power to distinguish illusion from reality, falsehood from truth, the relative from the absolute. The deepest objective of secularism is precisely to "liberate" man from the order by which he is submissive to his Creator, to "emancipate" him from his existential source, to "change" the system of truth in which he lives into a factual and mental relativity. Thus an inevitable consequence is, not an accrued perspicuity in the imaginative life of man, but on the contrary an ever growing opacity.

Love is one of the first victims of the growing confusion provoked by secularization. It is not a system or an article of faith which could be integrated and defended in the cadre of orthodoxy. Nor is it a doctrine to thrust forward in opposition to other theories. This is why it is more vulnerable and more exposed to alternations and falsifications than anything else in the world of spiritual concepts. Just as crustaceans, at the time of shedding their shells, are easy prey to rapacious animals of the sea, love is a choice booty for the falsifiers serving the cause of secularization. In the first place, this falsification consists in passing under silence and in effacing from human consciousness the essence and source of love.

All creation, all production is a gift. Love is such a gift. As all that is created and produced is, in the final analysis, traced back to its divine source, it is God who is the source of all love. God is love, and this is true in relation to His creation. Love is an "aspect" of the divine reality. God "becomes" love by his manifestation, for in the created work He manifests and objectivizes Himself. The creation is simultaneously expression and object of His love.

The creation is a gift, but also a possession. It is an incessant flux coming from the Creator Himself, but also a community in that God in His omnipotence includes all His created work. Love in its divine origin has a double scope as it is at the same time both gift and possession. But this does not imply duality. This latter is to be found only on the terrestrial level of love. God's love is one and indivisible and therefore cannot be divided into a duality. If we say that it is double, that must be understood in the sense that God, for the one part, manifests Himself in creation; and for the other, He "is" in the created work as universal spirituality. Loving Father, He always watches over His work and over his children on earth. He possesses, keeps, and protects the created work in order to restore to the source of love, when the times will have been accomplished, that which love has created. This cyclic aspect of creation is thus tied to love, which finds there its perspective of eternity even in terrestrial manifestation: love "changes not" even from the terrestrial point of view.

The created work is a cosmos, an order. As love is an essential element in creation, it cannot therefore be outside this order. On the contrary, it is integrated in it, and this is why it is possible for us to live it in an objective fashion. Love is not some sort of pseudo-metaphysical "fire," nor some current of sentimental energy passing through the world. Nor, certainly, is it a "natural force" which "liberates" man and gives him the subjective right to elevate himself above all legal order. Even less is it a legislative power permitting man to say that "love is always right." It does not justify a pretended liberty to "suppress frontiers." It does not legitimize chaos. It is a part of the created order; it is in defense of this order, not in its destruction, that love is realized.

The love of the Creator is one and indivisible, but, on the terrestrial plane of reflection, we find duality, that precisely which differentiates the Heavens from the earth. Certainly there exists a "love of self" of which the young Narcissus is the prototype in Greek mythology, but something is morbid there which is already figured in the legend: Narcissus, lovingly contemplating his own image, languishes and dies. The ultra romantic and always tragically vain efforts to reinterpret the myth by making of narcissism an "experience of oneself" confirm the truth that love is participation.

In this regard terrestrial love is faithful to its celestial model, being at once gift and possession. But it is a duality, a tension between two poles which persists the more, not only in that they unite, but in that they preserve their independence. Love thus becomes simultaneously community and experience of oneself, union and polarized tension.

The primordial manifestation of all terrestrial love is procreation. In nature as in the human species, there goes on without ceasing this process founded on the duality man-woman, these two beings who are endlessly drawn the one to the other, meeting and uniting without, however, the element of tension which separates them being abolished. When Goethe speaks of the eternal feminine which attracts us, he expresses his opinion that love pertains to the being of creation, that the feminine and the masculine are archetypal forces which condition the perpetuation of the created work and from which flows constantly a new production of life.

We encounter divine as well as terrestrial love, and this on two levels of manifestation. To the procreative love between man and woman is added the love of parents for the fruits of their procreation. This latter is hierarchic encounter between the superior and the inferior, while procreative love is encounter between equals. The hierarchical aspect is the form of love linking Heaven and earth. Such is the divine love which descends into creation and is reflected in the relationships of parents with their children. But in the created work, production follows a horizontal course; it is the encounter between man and woman, or in the Vedantic terms, between *Purusha* and *Prakriti*.

Can we then speak of superior and inferior love, carnal and immaterial, of Eros and Agapé? Is it advisable to establish such categories? First, it is necessary to remember that the love of God is universal and includes all. It penetrates all, even earthly love under its most sensual and sexual forms, for the divine love also comprises archetypes which are the models of earthly love and of the masculine and feminine principles. Thus terrestrial love, even in its most carnal form is prefigured in the divine order. The organic world, vegetables and animals and humans, accomplish on the terrestrial plane the work of divine creation, and it is in the same manner that we continue this work by our toil.

The struggle against the "flesh" is not an expression of a duality of love. Love experienced on earth does not suffer from a tragic and irremediable division between Eros and Agapé. Certainly one rightly speaks of a more or less elevated quality of love—it is a question then of the hierarchic and vertical order—just as one designates it with just as much reason as platonic or physical. But it is not there that the differences in principle reside. All is united in the energy of the divine creation, just as the Christian cross is the reunion of two branches, the one vertical and the other horizontal. If not thus, how would family life be possible? How could the "carnal" union of spouses combine with the "disincarnated" love of parents for their children?

The important fact is that divine love penetrates all earthly love, even in its most carnal manifestations. This is why the combat against the flesh is not the expression of some irreducible dualism of love. On the contrary, it is destined precisely to oppose itself to such a dualism, and to hinder the creature from withdrawing from its Author, to impede earthly love being "liberated" from its celestial source. The love of God encompasses all, such is the final response to the question. Even the apostle Paul, so wroth against the flesh, proclaims that this latter is ennobled by the Spirit: "What! know ye not that your body is the temple of the Holy Spirit which is in you, which ye have of God, and that ye are not your own?" (1 Cor. 6:10).

Love is one, but its forms of manifestation are multiple. It is manifested under aspects and forms of the most varied kinds. The "pleasures of the flesh" are not a tragic and culpable destiny which hangs over humanity. The most sensual enjoyment of love does not in itself comport a shadow of sin and of guilt. On the contrary, it is in holding that there are two essential forms of love—tragic division realized especially by the Calvinist sects—that one removes the possibilities of "ennobling the flesh" spiritually.

Certainly love is not egotistical. Nevertheless one cannot say that the object of love would be "lacking in interest" or unworthy of being sought. For love tends at the same time to give itself and to possess. Union and relationship are not renunciation of oneself nor the effacement of him who loves. God does not efface Himself in his uninterrupted creation, any more than man and woman lose the characteristics of their sex when they unite with one another physically and corporeally. On the contrary, the inclination to possession can merge into a force that apparently carries the marks of egotism and disorder. But its object is situated outside self, and this object is union. The fusion of the self in a relationship with the other, of possession and gift, is something that is designated, not without reason, as the mystery of love: as in an alchemical process, the apparently contrary elements are blended into a creative union.

Every created being has a beginning and must have an end. If a created thing had to endure eternally, that would signify that it would escape from the omnipotence of God to establish its own order, independent of the absolute character of eternity. The divine omnipotence would be traduced. When we recognize this omnipotence we recognize at the same time that the created is found in a cyclic process, with a continual return to its source. The human relation with the Creator then assumes a double aspect: on the one part, we thank Him for the life we have received and for all that is given in our terrestrial life; and for the other part we aspire to communion, to the rediscovery which definitively constitutes the termination of the cycle.

This is why the philosophy of Plato sees in the human aspiration for the Supreme Good not an empty speculation, but a wisdom drawn, as he himself informs us, from more ancient sources. It is on the basis of the same wisdom and with the same certitude that Aristotle founded his doctrine of natural process: there is an immovable center that puts all into movement, in the same manner that the beloved object sets into motion him who loves; it is to this which philosophy has given the famous appellation *kinei hos eremenon.** This fundamental idea is found with Plato, with St. Augustine, as well as with the mystics and theologians of the Middle Ages: man tends towards a goal which is divine and with which he aspires to be united. It is not the man who "wills," it is the goal which elicits the aspiration.

There is in our terrestrial life a place where these multiple aspects of love converge as in the focus of a lens; that is to say, the family. It is the point where the love between man and woman meets that which exists between parents and children. It is the nucleus whence germinates all the life of love; and in that love it becomes the sanctuary where the child, for the first time, encounters the love of Heaven as well as that of the earth, which surrounds his education. It is a microcosmic circle which reflects the macrocosmic totality. On the level of terrestrial manifestation it is the point of crystallization of divine love.

Even if the family is infinitely more than a simple bourgeois institution, its social importance is none the less for being so. Thanks to education within its cadre, the new generation acquires on the personal level a consciousness of identity and on the social level a consciousness of community. The family is also a school for life in society and through the family the child learns to protect the weak and the disabled, to assume responsibilities, to show respect, as well as to practice solidarity and mutual aid. It is the place where the younger generation encounters paternity and fraternity which

---

*The Greek *kinei hos eremenon* signifies, in the words of Aristotle (*Metaphysics* 12.7 [1072b]): "The final cause, then, produces motion as being loved, but all other things move by being moved."—Translator.

it experiences not as literary phenomena nor as clichés on posters at public meetings or in the texts of resolutions, but as realities of the familial community[31]

There is, in the Kingdom of Man, much uncertainty and even confusion on the subject of man's situation vis-à-vis love. It has been pretended for generations that humanity was going to become a single great fraternal community. Liberty and equality must open the way to fraternity. But it has never been shown convincingly where the spiritual force was coming from that would permit the race to surmount the egoism of profane and sensual men, and thus prepare the advent of universal human love. Nevertheless, the idea that a humanity deprived of paternity might even so reach a universal community of love has not ceased to engender hope as men anticipate the great projects for the establishment of a world of security, well-being, equality, and justice.

Institutional revolutions and radical reforms, as well as the education which is inspired by them, apparently, are supposed to be the royal way leading to this fraternity full of love. But another way to reach this goal is also proposed. And it is here that Sigmund Freud intervenes as principal guide with the libido relationship between men and women. The source of all love is not God, but the carnal nature of man himself. Freud supresses the hierarchic relationship even in the terrestrial sense. His work contains no allusion to the love between parents and children. On the contrary, one of his fundamental notions is the alleged Oedipus complex: the mother becomes a "sexual object" for her son and the father a "rival" with respect to this "object." Thus the parents, reduced to

[31]A beautiful description of the traditional Chinese family was published almost a century ago by Tcheng-Ki-Tong, military attaché of China then posted at Paris, in an article in the *Revue des Deux Mondes*. The Chinese family, he says, develops into a community, a great family comprising hundreds of members, a "sort of religious order subject to fixed rules." Under the authority of the oldest, all resources are gathered together to be divided equitably and if a member of the family falls ill or is out of work, the others intervene. The family obeys an order of equality and fraternity, "great words which are inscribed in the hearts and not on walls." Tcheng-Ki-Tong, "La Chine et les chinois," *Revue des Deux Mondes* 63 (15 May 1884): 278ff.

the same level, become objects for the libidinous inclinations of the new generation of children. Love then becomes "unidimensional." King Eros exercises an absolute sovereignty on all levels. King Oedipus has shown us the line to follow: that which we desire is to kill our fathers. King Marx has shown us the way to collective parricide, which is revolution. His spiritual cousin, Sigmund Freud, would teach us individual parricide.

Even if the Oedipus doctrine must naturally be interpreted in a symbolic sense, it nevertheless gives expression to the ungoverned satisfaction of libidinous inclinations. Is humanity, therefore, to be given up to a sexual war without mercy? In no way. The prophets of sexual liberation have quite different aims. He who finds a libidinous partner in love goes beyond the narrow limits of his selfhood when he is sexually united with another creature, or so it is pretended. This union is an act of peace and fraternity, of human reconciliation. Eros becomes the divinity of peace and fraternity. Divine love, and that of earthly parents, have no business in this context. Orthodoxy, dogmas, rules of morality are only obstacles provoking neurotic troubles. Freud proclaims, contrariwise, that the free libidinous experience of free individuals contains the germs of a relaxed, peaceful, and harmonious social life. This is the gospel of sexual democracy and sexual pacifism.[32]

The views of Freud on the problems of human life in common are in no way simple. He often expresses, and in a surprising manner, an accentuated pessimism. But his fixation on carnal love, the libido, is and remains central. In his suite have come generations of enthusiastic combatants for sexual democracy, doctrine of the free practice of the instinctive life between equal humans which, we are assured, is the way leading to the great community of men. Just as Marxism had declared that the final object of communism was work in free association, sexual radicalism proclaims that free libidinous association is the way to human harmony.

---

[32]See particularly: Sigmund Freud, *Massenpsychologie und Ich-Analyse*, Gesammelte Werke 12, pp. 112ff.

Whether one chooses the one or the other of these ways, that of institutional revolution in combination with a strictly egalitarian education, or that of the god of Eros, both are confronted with the same dilemma. It is believed possible to "create" love, and awaken to life something that is not found in the sensory life where one lives. Love exists, but not there where the moderns seek it. It is in its divine source, and in the world he finds it who knows how to draw from that source his strength and inspiration.

If one chooses the way of revolution, one places oneself at the point of view of collective egoism. If one gives oneself to the revolution or to the sexual life, the point of departure can be only that of the man egotistically bound to his sensory desires. No love, and no community animated by love, can be born from this egoism, for love exists already, as well as community, and that because we are all children of the same Father. This community does not become a reality except when we find this paternity and acknowledge it.

The Kingdom of Man is a social order without love. It is obliged to have recourse to growing numbers of laws and ordinances, to threats and reprisals, in order to maintain the cohesion of its troops when all the seductions of the all providential State no longer suffice. One cannot avoid noting the disappearance of all true fraternity, as well as the simple and daily sentiment of solidarity, of helpfulness and of solicitude. Let us not embellish the past. The history of humanity overflows with familiar conflicts and fratricidal struggles. Where can one find the community, the family, responding perfectly to ideal desiderata? Even if the family is presently decadent one has no reason to forecast a future for human relations envisaging, not only that the family is placed in question as an institution but that it is openly menaced with annihilation. For where there is no longer love nor charity, the door is open to brutality. Such is human nature.

Again, let us look at a form of life that is totally different from that which love wants to realize on the level of human relations. Let us look at its extreme opposite, ascetic isolation. Is not asceticism in conflict with love and with love's plenary fulfillment? Cannot one compare the ascetic with a sick man, a voluntary invalid? In appearance, he cuts himself off from the expression of love which, from the terrestrial point of view, is the most engaging and generous—the family. He remains apart from paternity and from a common life with the other sex. Thus love does not enter his life, neither under its hierarchic aspect, nor under its egalitarian aspect in the union of man and woman. Is the ascetic, therefore, the negator of all love?

These questions are the more significant in that asceticism is always presented with the pretention of representing an elevated terrestrial form of divine love. Asceticism is encountered in worship, in sacerdotal life, and in charitable activities exercised in the name of religion. No one can deny that it is a question here of ascetical forms of love on this earth. That must lead us to ask ourselves if love manifested here below does not have a dimension other than those that are expressed under the hierarchic and egalitarian aspects.

Asceticism is the third aspect. It is neither gift nor possession, but abstention from the expression of love through the flesh. It is submission to the divine love and at the same time aspiration to communicate this love on the terrestrial level without undergoing the influence of the flesh. It is not negation of carnal love, nor of any element of earthly life as such. Asceticism does not proceed from a dualist conception that envisages a superior existence "without sin" and an inferior world consisting of "sinners." The ascetic holds himself apart from the "world," but he does not deny it. The world is no more sinful for him than it is for others who live in it and enjoy terrestrial love to the full. The ascetic attitude is a confirmation—even if in negative terms—of earthly love, and not its negation. It is a fundamental error to see in asceticism a comportment that is hostile to material life, an error which constantly leads to the confusion of asceticism with putitanism.

Human love is participation. Divine love is also participation in the sense that God loves His created work; but divine love is, in its essence, a totality. It is eternal, immutable, absolute, having nothing relative in it. God "is" love. It is this absolute, eternal, and immutable love that the ascetic, in his imperfection, seeks to manifest on earth. It is of less importance to know if this takes the form of eremitic or cenobitic isolation, or of charitable action.

Cannot one say, finally, that all love bears a mark of asceticism? All profound and authentic love, whether it is in the flesh or not, is an "engagement" which is prolonged far beyond one's own person. Love is "blind," it is said, and that indicates that the "engagement" is combined with an abandonment of one's own interests, a devotedness, a sacrifice, a gift, all qualities of disinterestedness. An animal satisfaction of his instincts in promiscuity becomes insupportable to man in the long run. Love in its biological and fleshly form is joined to the spiritual, which not only "ennobles the flesh" but even abstains from the satisfaction of its immediate instinctive impulses. In that abstention, in that ennoblement, man acquires the possibility of raising his attention towards this love which reunites the fleshly and the immaterial in the source from which come all things and to which all must return.

Chapter 12
JUSTICE

When Jesus exhorted us to seek first the Kingdom of God and His justice, that certainly does not have an exclusively earthly significance. At bottom, justice, like love, is an aspect of the divine order. Just as love is a source from which gushes forth the stream manifesting the creation of God in its most elevated form, justice is a transcendent guarantee giving the assurance that not anything created is submitted to a merely arbitrary treatment. It gives the lie to all those doctrines affirming the predominance of hazard in existence. It is thus a *suum cuique*, to each his own, to which all created existence is subordinated, a "judgment" from which existence itself cannot escape.

In this situation it is important for us humans, primarily to never forget God and, thereby, to guard the consciousness of being subject to the divine omnipotence; to consider the Day of Judgment which awaits us, where we will be judged on a balance of justice; and thirdly, to know that the judgment will not be an execution, but a just evaluation of what our eternal life must be. The Judgment is a conclusion of the short existence on earth, limited in time and space, and the introduction of an eternity independent of any existential form.

Justice penetrates all things in the original creation and is manifest at all levels. When we say that it is an aspect of the divine order, that is to say that it is expressed first of all in cosmic manifestation, in the total creation. Justice is then a balance, or the equilibrium of the created which interdicts a macrocosmic chaos and which on the microcosmic level impedes the reign of hazard.[33]

Symbolically, the goddess of justice is represented holding a balance in her hand. To this equilibrium and therefore to this superior justice, men have often had to submit themselves at great pain that fills them with bitterness. Through the centuries pious and just men have asked themselves why not only the fields of their unbelieving neighbor have been struck by hail and infertility, but their own as well? Why are the sufferings and the trials of the world distributed in such an unjust fashion? The ordinary response is: because God wants to try us. This is true, but it is incomplete, because it clarifies only the microcosmic aspect. It is more important to provide a response corresponding to the macrocosmic aspect: because creation is an order, an equilibrium, which we humans, with our sufferings and our earthly concerns, do not have the right to question. Such also is the content of the response made to Job by Elihu, son of Barachel. Or, as the French mathematician Joseph Bertrand said in a more profane and facetious form: if it rains all day on the Place du Carrousel, all the paving stones are equally wet.

Justice has a transcendent source and is manifest cosmically as an equilibrium opposing itself to chaos and to hazard. But it also has a third and microcosmic aspect. The individual lives in an order of justice and he must correctly receive the exhortation which relates thereto. The heart is the point where justice resides. It is in the

---

[33]It is interesting to see the manner in which profane science, referring to anterior speculations relative to what has been called political arithmetic, was preoccupied in the last century with the hazard versus order problem. The Belgian statistician, Adolphe Quetelet, in a series of works, believed he found a stability in human life in the form of a mean relating not only to the length of the body, its weight, its strength or its rapidity, but even to the moral and intellectual characteristics of men. Setting aside the scientific value of these speculations, the conclusion of the author is nevertheless interesting: "How man is subject, whether he will or not, to divine laws, and with what regularity he accomplishes them!" Adolphe Quetelet, *Anthropométrie ou mesure des différents facultés* (Brussels, 1871), p. 21.

heart that we must preserve the equilibrium which corresponds to the harmonic unity of the entire creation. If all, good and bad, are struck by pestilence and famine, this is not an expression of injustice. This latter arises only from the moment when man arises with rebellion in his heart to contest this superior order and pretends to be his own legislator.

No normal man remains passive in the grip of suffering and difficulties. Everyone defends himself—and must do so—against suffering, just as difficulties must be surmounted. That is in no way in contradiction with divine justice. It is when one negates the superior order, and when man refuses to recognize a superior power and even a superior justice, that injustice arises in the heart of man. This rupture of equilibrium is the prelude to the deviation of the Kingdom of Man, far from truth and life. This is also what Job finally understood: "I was he who mixed up thy counsels by senseless utterances. Also I have spoken without intelligence of marvels which are beyond me and of which I am ignorant" (Job 42:3).

There is a close relation between love and justice. Both are parts of the created order, but each represents a different aspect. Justice is tied to equilibrium, love to grace. The end, for us humans, is not only judgment. With the latter, grace and mercy also intervene. Our actions are placed on the pans of a balance. This is why justice is, with its *suum cuique* [to each his own], the expression of an egalitarian aspect of weighing. Grace in turn, as a force acting by love in existence, touches us vertically as a ray of the "sun of grace."

When we say that "love is blind," that has not only a profane signification but also one that is justified: on the earthly level we allow ourselves to be blinded easily by a passion so that we refuse to see the faults that the object of our love may have. But the "blindness" of love also has a more profound sense. Just as the sun dazzles us by its rays, we are incapable of "seeing" the rays of the sun of love and grace which come to us from above. In the same manner, one says that justice is blind in one eye. When the "goddess of justice" is represented with a blindfold over one eye, that obviously means that terrestrial justice pronounces its sentences with the narrow view of the "one-eyed," which is inherent in all that is earthly and therefore imperfect. But this view of the single eye is also an expression of the truth that the superior justice is unconditional and does not look towards that which might be a compromise or a modification of the *suum cuique* in the supraterrestrial sense. Our pair of eyes is one symbol expressing the duality of our human existence. But it is the "eye" of God which sees, and we must also discern the symbolic character of this "unique" eye of justice.

Love is one of the great victims of the modern process of alteration and destruction. One can say as much of justice. The point of departure is always the same: individual man. For in the Kingdom of Man, there are "no other gods but me," and utilizing all means at his disposition the human being must conquer his position of power. And when it is a question of love and of justice, the premise is posed: there is no superior love, no superior justice. The center of the one and of the other is the individual self, sensual man devoted to his own self-interest. The point of departure is egoism.

How, in these conditions, can justice be established? How, in this crossfire of sensory forces and interests, can any kind of justice prevail? To respond to these questions, let us return for a moment to one of the principal masters of the thought of the system, Rousseau. Let us listen attentively to what he says. In all his writings one perceives a fundamental note: self-pity. It is himself that he loves. In this autistic world, he encounters his own fragility, his weaknesses, his morbid tendencies, his torments, and his pains. There is no possibility for him to view himself objectively as a creature dependent on a merciful Father. Because for the deist, the Creator has retired and confined himself behind a celestial curtain. Rousseau is delivered up to himself and to his sufferings. Then he creates a religious pseudo-world of which the center is the temple of sentimentality which is called the human heart. It is there that he barricades himself in his autism, enclosing himself in his incommensurable self-pity. And it is in this sentimental temple, the human heart, that he elaborates the new "esoterism."

Rousseau, with an infallible self-assurance, seized the essential. The center of man is the heart—it is there that the insoluble conflict is to be found that opposes Rousseau to the much more cerebral encyclopedists. He himself situates the basis in the heart. It is this latter which he "conquers" and transforms into a temple of sentimentality. The heart is no longer the Kingdom of God which is "within you." It is the autistic headquarters of the Kingdom of Man. Nature reigns within the heart, and Nature is good in herself. "At the bottom" of this heart, in this "natural" temple, according to Rousseau, man is pure and good; there, not only our sensory but also our moral foundation is to be found. Secularized man has "conquered" love and justice.

Rousseau, one of the greatest and most influential among the seducers and poisoners of the West, however, clearly distinguishes the other aspect of man which must henceforth possess the earth. Power is also necessary to man. But the thirst for power, can it be reconciled with man's innate "natural" goodness? Yes, Rousseau considers, for when we are weak we are evil. Let us become strong, and we will become good. That is one of the fundamental articles of faith of his *Emile*.* All submission, all subordination, all servility arouses malice in the human mind. It is only when he is free, strong, loosed from his bonds that man becomes good and accomplishes good actions. And this is a message addressed to all humanity.

From that time onward, the image that Rousseau formed of humanity appears in its principal traits. In the heart resides sentimental self-pity, but also pure and innocent Nature; and with Nature, the love of justice. Nevertheless, to reach this goodness, this purity, this justice, and this love, man must be equally free, strong, without bonds, "neither the lord nor the slave of anyone." He must at the same time, therefore, have power. How to resolve this problem? In only one way: by equality. "When Adam dug and Eve spun, who then was a gentleman?" was already sung in the Middle Ages; and this age-old dream must now be realized. One must not seek justice "above," but realize it here below, in earthly equality.

**Emile, ou de l'éducation*, 1762, was a sort of didactic novel and the source of much progressive education theory. Translator's note.

Self-pity and the desire for power constitute an alliance on which justice rests. But this base, in the final analysis, is nothing other than human egoism. Is this really the situation? All the measures of social providence in the modern states, all the international actions of solidarity and of assistance, all the efforts destined to ameliorate living conditions of the so-called underdeveloped peoples, would all that have been possible without a motive other than cold egoism?

The objection carries some weight, but we must first of all remember that the Kingdom of Man has two poles: the individual bearer of the human egoism, and the collectivity—bearer of the egalitarian order. In this collectivity, devoid of charity, and where, consequently, morality has only a single dimension, it is a question of resolving double problems. For the one part, no one can be stronger than I—and the self defends itself against a horde of wolves—and for the other, no one can be weaker. In such conditions all difference is a menace, even on the part of the weak—if not especially on the part of the weak—which may be directed against me. This is why an important element of the fundamental system of social security consists in eliminating all backwardness in an egalitarian regime.

Such is one of the essential rules of all these tendencies. Equality, as the relationship of power, is an equivalent of terror, neither more nor less. But power, it has been said, is only one aspect of the picture. The other is self-pity. Moderns form a curious mixture: on the one hand, a conceited and aggressive desire for power and, on the other, a sentimental compassion towards their own weakness and confusion. It is this last psychic component which gives such a pronounced emotional note to the life of profane man. Amidst all the glorification of democratic liberty and the exercise of power by the citizenry one perceives an undeniable tendency to spread and, so to speak, to socialize self-pity.

Does this lead to a true compassion of a universal compass? To respond to that question, we must first note that this pity, individual or universal, contains an important psychic component; the fear of suffering. He who seeks the Kingdom of God and His justice knows that suffering is an integral part of our imperfect world and that, in this world, we cannot avoid it—which would mean wanting to run from our own shadow. Nevertheless, the chorus leaders of modernism, among their great objectives, take upon themselves that of the abolition of suffering, for their point of departure is sensory and egotistical man, and that which is negatively expressed as the abolition of suffering implies, positively, the well-being and the material and psychic satiety of the individual. It is the all-providential State which furnishes the guarantee of all this on the collective level.

The fear of suffering and the efforts to eliminate it provide the emotional base for the order of profane justice. This must not be confused with compassion. This latter is man's disposition to go out of his own ego and to place himself in the position of his neighbor. One cannot be further from this attitude than are the inhabitants of the Kingdom of Man. Egalitarianism excludes charity because the former is not renunciation but revendication. It implies the quantitative control of things. At the beginning and at the end of all this system is found the aspiration of the egotistical individual to satisfy his needs for sensory enjoyments. The existence of man becomes then, individually as well as collectively, a defense of his own well-being and not a disposition to sacrifice and renounce it. If he wishes the well-being of all, this is neither from compassion nor from charity, but because it appears to him as the one solid guarantee of his own individual well-being.

Even so, compassion and charity exist in the world, and they inspire works of great value. It is a human duty and obligation to assuage distress. But it is not by following modernist ways that one can keep true compassion alive. These ways are false because those who map them out believe that the material well-being of humanity is the highest expression of justice. One must not forget that there exists a true and a false presentation of justice. That the second attracts a greater number of men, of whom many are assuredly animated by "good intentions," changes nothing in the affair. A false doctrine does not become true by the fact that it gains more adherents.

Chapter 13
THE VOICE OF CONSCIENCE

The Kingdom of Man has made the great and proud promise of liberating us from feelings of guilt. For if man is a free being and untrammeled by any bonds, being "neither the lord nor the slave of anyone," at the same time he becomes free of the bondage to which he had been subject for thousands of years, to a superior power demanding of him accounts for all that he had done or not done. Henceforth, responsible only to himself, he is the free and happy creature who "says yes to life" and accepts from her all that she can offer him. Then there is no longer any place for any feeling of guilt, so one considers. The notion of sin must be effaced from the world and there must be no more torments of conscience, nor despondency resulting from a fault committed.

Before this stimulating perspective, the reformers have lost no time, in the fields of education, social ethics, and criminology, in preparing the ways of this new existence "free of guilt." Man is naturally good, as one continues to preach, and it is the role of education to let individual energies freely exercise their self-regulating activity according to this innate natural goodness. On the social level men will be equal and this equality will furnish the guarantee that the natural goodness will not be corrupted and that the realization of oneself will not be thwarted.

Consequently, offenses cannot be anything else but the effect of a series of unhappy circumstances, unless they result directly from a false and unjust social system. Man being fundamentally good, it is a matter of making his life conform to that fund of natural goodness. The offense is not therefore the "fault" of man who, in principle, is not "culpable." The fault is then that of society which then must be transformed by revolutionary or reformatory means; or else the offense is inadaptation, the taking of a wrong path or the failure to fit the individual into the social collectivity, in which case the necessary amends and work of readaptation must be effected, as if it were a question of the interruption of an electric current.

One knows only too well how these romantic aberations have led us to a situation of crisis—spiritually, morally, pedagogically, and even criminologically. A formidable seed is beginning to ripen. This is the implacable result of a denial, of a refusal to recognize that we are created beings, children of the same Father to whom we are indebted for all in our lives. The recognition that we owe Him is tied to the consciousness that, for all that we receive constantly and daily from our Creator, we have before Him the situation of a debtor.

We are unable to "reimburse" that which we have received and do receive daily from our Creator. Our terrestrial imperfection makes it quite impossible for us to "settle our debts." The consciousness of being in debt is above all else our condition. Our debt is an existential fact. Sacrifice is an expression of it. Ever since there have been men on earth, some have always been found to offer themselves in sacrifice to a superior power, because this consciousness of an existential debt has always existed.

But no sacrifice is ever great enough. For in the plate of the balance is placed the gift that is our life, with all that we receive in addition. It is not possible for us to load the other plate as heavily, whatever we might put there. One cannot make the temporal the equivalent of eternity, nor the relative the equal of the absolute, nor place existential imperfection on the same level as that which is holy. Man remains forever charged with his debt to the Creator. The words of confession, stating in effect that "we have sinned every day," express nothing other than this fundamental fact of our debt which, in our imperfection, grows each day and each hour. For, in the final analysis, sin is nothing other than existence. And when we say that sin increases in the world, this is not an expression of pessimism nor a sentimental dramatization, but simply a manner of recognizing our existential imperfection.

It is here that the modern prophets commit one of their numerous and calamitous errors when they announce that man shall be comforted and happy, free and strong, while seeking to deny his debt. This proclamation certainly has not raised up a new human generation free from neuroses; it has been conducive to exactly the opposite result. For the equilibrium between the two trays of the balance is found in the interior life of our soul. And in order to reach this point, our sacrifices on the human level do not suffice. Something more is demanded of us, an avowal of our dependence, a recognition of what we have received and still receive, as well as an acceptance of the grace of God which surpasses all intelligence. Only then will the balance between the two trays of the scale be realized.

The negation of this truth is one of the principal sources of psychic disorder and of growing neurotic troubles. But secularized men more and more accept neurosis as an inevitable situation, as if psychic suffering in the world was a misery resulting from determinism. Against this pessimism that arises in the midst of all the profane promises of liberty and happiness, there is room for reaction. The world is what it is, full of imperfections and miseries. But in face of this, a resigned and passive attitude would be as indolent as false. It is slack because it would have us close our eyes before our own insufficiencies and lead us to think that we have no obligation to ourselves. It is false because the existence of evil is one thing while the fight against evil is something else. It must be that scandals arrive, but woe to him by whom the scandal comes. These are words of Christ which we must keep in our memory. Nor is sin a simple notion. Failures, deficiencies, forgetfulness, complacency are part of our daily life to the point that we are aware only with difficulty of these continual expressions of our weakness. There are also conscious faults of which we are aware not only when we actually commit them, but which we have projected and planned. The will then enters: we have consciously chosen. There are, yet again, sins which do not exclude piety, faith, and the intention to obey the commandments, but we are too weak to hinder the will from engaging us in unjust ways. And one can cite the sins that not only are deliberate and prepared, but integrated in a conscious negation of the good; it is then the most profound sin, the inversion. Evil is declared good, and vice versa. This is satanism. Truth and falsehood have been inverted and Satan is proclaimed sovereign.

Do the inhabitants of the Kingdom of Man have the possibility of extricating themselves from all this? The question is grave, for the fate of the modern world depends upon it. If man could throw off his debt, then he might become the free, happy, and harmonious creature that it has been pretended could be made of him, then all consciousness of God would be eliminated. The great banquet of life would commence.

Nothing, however, presently leads us to think that things may take such a turn. One is witness, rather, to a rupture of psychic equilibrium. The new generations are raised in ignorance or in growing forgetfulness of the divine order. They are taught to conceive existence as limited to the world of sensible things. They are pushed to break every rapport of responsibility towards their surroundings. It is thus that one pretends to liberate them from all ideas of sin and of debt, which, one thinks, must stifle the voice of conscience. These new generations then would only have to take in hand their own responsibilities.

At first view, that might seem a light and agreeable charge to bear. In reality, it is a terrible burden that is placed on their shoulders. Our existential imperfection cannot be denied, dissimulated, "forgotten." It is always there and comes to mind continually. The intellective consciousness can be led to the limit of elimination, but it does not allow itself to be completely effaced. One can give new names to sin, to responsibility, and to conscience. But sin, responsibility, and conscience remain and always make themselves known afresh to our attention. Who lightens the weight of our failings, who pardons sin, who stills the voice of conscience? Contemporary secularized man can count only on himself. He is master on earth and therefore he alone has the power to respond to his own acts.

Then a trial proceeding is opened, that of man against himself. Modern literature gives an account of this, as in Baudelaire, Kafka, Sandemose, or Camus. Man is here both plaintiff and defendant, accuser and advocate, judged and judge. "I am the wound and the blade, the victim and the executioner," exclaimed Baudelaire in his despair. And Camus, in his novel, *The Fall*, adds with a bitter irony: "Do not wait for the last judgment. It takes place every day."

In his own depths, man preserves the intellective consciousness of his true relationship with his Creator. He will never be able to eliminate it. This is why the consciousness of existential imperfection remains and, therefore, an existential responsibility. It is this consciousness of insufficiency which constitutes such an important part of the psychic equilibrium of man. In one of the trays of the balance we have the love and the infinite grace of God; we place in the other the consciousness of this love and of this grace with the recognition of all that which has been given to us, as well as the consciousness of the debt we have towards our Creator.

It is this spiritual equilibrium which the Kingdom of Man upsets. Its prophets exhort us to reject our feelings of insufficiency, to eliminate the notion of sin, assuring us that in this way one will come to health and strength. In reality it is the contrary. The rupture of equilibrium produces two results. First, it leads to solitude. One of the causes of the solitude in which contemporary man lives is the severance of communication with his Creator, of which the sentiment of guilt is the expression. Man then finds himself existentially isolated. Then this rupture of equilibrium, which cannot be eliminated, causes the awareness of guilt to be shifted into the interior of the individual, which marks the beginning of the proceedings which man brings against himself. Nevertheless, the feelings of guilt do not diminish, but on the contrary grow. For there is no longer anyone with whom one can be reconciled. There is no one to accord forgiveness.

Far from offering a way towards spiritual health, secular efforts to "liberate" humanity from feelings of guilt lead rather to psychic disorders and suffering. How can the progressive prophets explain that in place of the announced state of harmony and happiness, one observes an unceasing augmentation of psychic misery and neurotic derangement? They can offer no response, for if they wanted to reply in a manner that corresponds with reality, they would perforce at the same time announce their own capitulation.

Chapter 14
TO BE LIKE CHILDREN

The Kingdom of Man is based on the belief that the human being must develop himself rationally and emotionally to such a degree that the entire world will be subject to him. To this belief is allied the idea that the needs of men, in principle inexhaustible, can be satisfied thanks to a continued "progress," to a "development" going from bottom to top. According to the prophets of secularization, this "progress" is not only material, but as the shadow follows the body, spiritual needs accompany those of the flesh and will be equally appeased.

It is under the sign of ideological pride that such ideas are spread abroad. This same pride leads to such blindness as the following: the children of secularization do not see that what they call "progress" and "development" is nothing other than the instability which, in its turn, is an expression of existential imperfection. They have forgotten that perfection, the Absolute, the immutable, pertain to God—and instability to the world. The capacity for change, so appreciated by the modern world, in reality carries the mark of imperfection, which latter resides precisely in that which is subject to this changeableness.

But one may object to the partisans of religion that they exalt with man that which is simplistic and spiritually destitute. What therefore is "poverty of spirit?" One can understand this in two ways. There exists a spiritual indigence for which the most vast erudition cannot compensate. It is a "deficiency disease" which, despite all the medico-social realizations of the system, generally passes unperceived, but which we certainly must not regard as incurable. Yet, spiritual poverty must be envisaged in its most profound sense: it is humble submission to a spirituality which is not part of our mental faculties, but which comes from above. Poverty, then, must not be interpreted as a deficiency nor as an indigence. It is an attitude of virtue expressing the total dependence of him who receives, as well as his gratitude for what is given him.

That is why it is said: "Blessed are the poor in spirit." There is no praise of indigence nor of ignorance. Nor is there found a penchant for making oneself a martyr psychologically. Poverty of spirit is at the source of the riches offered to the man who extricates himself from the mental obstacles constituted by presumption and pride. It is at the antipodes of the former, and this is why in all spiritual life it occupies a place of such eminence among the virtues. It is not by accident that Jesus mentioned it at the beginning of the Sermon on the Mount.

Nevertheless, the temptation exists to interpret it as an exemption from spiritual effort. Just as the secularized world consists of two opposed tendencies, for the one part an exaggerated faith in the powers of reason and its fruits, principally science; and for the other part, the inclination of covetous man to satisfy his vegetative needs, there exists also in spiritual tradition two apparently contradictory elements. From one side we have an exacting tendency towards maturity in order to be able to understand the truth and to live in conformity with it. On the other side, we must be "as children."

The process of maturation, biological in the vegetative and animal kingdoms, mental in the human species, has always incited man to consider with an exaggerated faith the "natural" possibilities of development. Humanity has always constructed many Towers of Babel, and no confusion of tongues has been able to hinder new generations from beginning again. That which is the most surprising in the French Revolution, remarks Alexis de Toqueville, is the credulity in relation to the possibilities of development of man. These recurrent miscarriages testify to nothing so much as to the deceitful character of the dream relative to human sovereignty and "autoregulation." Biological and mental maturation are a part of the created order, but nothing more than a part. For this created order reposes on the equilibrium of the forces of existence, and its task is to bring us back to order in our constant and presumptuous over-evaluation of ourselves. The created work of God is an order, a cosmos of which the first precept implies that "the tree shall not grow to the heavens," that our dominant position on earth is limited, in time as in space, to our mission as viceroy.

The process of maturation leading man to the point at which he can assume responsibility for himself and for his acts is an indispensable aspect of our situation on earth. When it is put in question, as for example when current egalitarian propaganda leads to infantile or symbiotic forms of social life which, deliberately or not, compromise the latter, that provokes a disorder in the cosmic equilibrium—with catastrophic consequences if one does not see to it in time. But it is in no way in contradiction with the Gospel exhortations engaging us to receive the truth as "little children," in the simplicity of our hearts.

The parable of the grain of mustard seed contains a universal precept. The "smallest of all the seed" symbolizes the microcosm, but this latter grows until it becomes a tree in the branches of which the birds of the air come to nest. This cosmic tree therefore grows sufficiently to receive the most elevated messages. Jesus wanted to show by this comparison in what manner maturity must be understood in its universal significance. But there is a temptation there to believe that the human being, in the same manner of the grain of mustard seed, can grow to the point of becoming the imposing tree which, by its own vigor, reaches the celestial truth. Would spiritual realization then be anything other than a human "autoregulation"? Jesus himself gave the response when his disciples came forward and asked: "Who is the greatest in the Kingdom of Heaven?" He called a child, placed him in the middle of them and said: "If you are not converted and become as one of these little children, you will not enter into the Kingdom of the Heavens."

It is to an adult man that Jesus addresses these words. He wanted to deflect the temptation that this man could experience of overestimating his own powers and of giving them a false orientation as does some existential theology with its "man come of age." This is not an exhortation to become infantile or to disarm the adult state that Jesus addresses to us. It is not an inert abandonment to the stage of prepubescent childhood—in the name of "fraternal" equality. Nor is it a question of the pedagogical regression of Rousseau, an attitude dully hostile to the adult world. For Jesus did not say: become children. He said: "He who humbles himself as this child is the greatest in the Kingdom of the Heavens." It is in this "as" that Jesus indicates what our effort must be.

Jesus responded to the question of the disciples in giving a little child as model. This response contains multiple aspects. In the child, we see weakness and incapacity. We see in him also innocent candor and confident hope. It is in that that the child constitutes a model. At the same time he represents the new birth, the creation that is always renewed, the cyclic return. That which always touches us with the little child, weak and incapable, soliciting indulgence and love, is the original paradisiacal purity—innocence. We must also perceive the cosmic totality in this primordiality, at the same time as the recall of our own inveteration and of the necessity of "becoming children" as our life approaches its end.

This is not to say that the Kingdom of God must be proclaimed only for men having attained a certain degree of maturity. The capacity to receive the words of divine truth is certainly not determined by one's cerebral volume. It is into the heart that the words of truth penetrate and there that they are understood, for it is there that the immortal spirit resides. This is why the little child is as "ripe" as the adult for the Kingdom of God.

He who humbles himself will be the greatest in the Kingdom of the Heavens, such is the response of Jesus. He aims thus especially at spiritual pride, first among mortal sins, which inexorably close the gates of heaven. And to give greater force to his utterance, He adds: "And whoever scandalizes one of these little ones who believe in me, it would be better for him if one attached around his neck a millstone and cast him into the sea." For if it is necessary to conduct our lives in such a manner as to become ripe and responsible beings, it is also and equally our responsibility to preserve in ourselves that which is innocent and pure as in the example of the child. The work of evil is to seduce and to destroy, and we are unable to thwart it. The world is not a paradise; it is an imperfection where evil has its place. "It must be that scandals come," said Jesus, "but woe to him by whom the scandal arrives."

It is our duty to grow and to become ripe, responsible, and reasonable men. We must make use of our reason and, according to our capacity, extend our knowledge. But that must not mask the view of the model which the child in his innocence constitutes. It is exactly in him that we meet creation in its totality; from the microcosmic point of view, he is the grain of mustard seed which must grow in order to become an imposing tree; cosmically, he is an expression of the uninterrupted process of creation, and, finally on the metacosmic level he represents the divine mercy which, ceaselessly, dispenses new life. We are able then to understand truly the words of the Son of Man concerning all of us: "Let the little children come unto me and do not hinder them, for of such is the Kingdom of God."

SELECTED BIBLIOGRAPHY

This is not a bibliography of works used by Dr. Lindbom in writing this book, though several if not all of the authors listed here are familiar to the author. The footnotes in the text will serve in part for a textual bibliography, but Dr. Lindbom's erudition is obviously much broader than the footnotes suggest. The Introduction by Roger Du Pasquier indicates some of the authors whose works were crucial as the author of *The Tares and the Good Grain* moved from the convinced socialist that he was to become a formidable and eloquent critic, showing up the internal contradictions and *degringolade* path of the godless socialist states and their background mentality which constitute the Kingdom of Man. The titles listed are recommended as having some relation, direct or indirect, to themes discussed in the text. Only works available in English language editions are given. These works are not of a popular nature and few would be found in any but major libraries, though several have appeared in paperback editions in the United States or in Britain and are still in print as of this writing.

Ananda K. Coomaraswamy. This scholar-writer was a master of English whose preferred publishing form was that of dense, highly concentrated papers or articles which more often than not appeared originally in obscure learned journals difficult to locate in any but the larger libraries. He addressed himself especially to the learned. Recently, two volumes of his collected papers have appeared under the auspices of the Bollingen Foundation (Princeton University Press), and these are entitled: *Coomaraswamy: Collected Papers*. 1 *Traditional*

Art and Symbolism, and 2 *Metaphysics*. A third volume completing the set consists of a biography of Coomaraswamy by Roger Lipsey.

Two noteworthy articles not included in the collection mentioned above, but which are of particular interest as theoretical background to the Lindbom book are "Spiritual Authority and Temporal Power in the Indian Theory of Government" (1942), and "Recollection, Indian and Platonic" (1944), both published as supplements to the *Journal of the American Oriental Society*. Also worth noting in this context is *The Bugbear of Literacy*, published in the early 1940s and again in 1979.

Rama P. Coomaraswamy. *The Destruction of the Christian Tradition*. London: Perennial Books,1981. A short history of the appalling debacle that has befallen the Roman Catholic Church from the time of Vatican II. Once the bulwark of Christianity, the once mighty and beloved Catholic Church seems well on its way to enshrining nothing more than a sinister cult of man. These events affecting the Catholic Church are themselves most disturbing signs of the times, and we need only examine these developments to appreciate that Lindbom's book is not overstated.

Gai Eaton. *King of the Castle, Choice and Responsibility in the Modern World*. London: The Bodley Head, 1977. The author states, or restates what it means to be man, as seen from the traditional perspective. He fits this profound understanding into the context of the modern, artificial, urban, industrial, socialistic society in which most Americans and Europeans must perforce live. The book then offers valuable counsel, explicit or implicit, as to how man can fulfill his God-given role in spite of multiple opposing pressures from all sides.

René Guénon. An author who wrote with almost mathematical precision, and whose works continue to be reprinted in France even though some of them originally appeared over fifty years ago. Those relating especially to the present Lindbom book are: *East and West*, *The Crisis of the Modern World*, *General Introduction to the Study of the Hindu Doctrines*, *The Symbolism of the Cross*, *Man and His Becoming according to the Vedanta*, and especially *The Reign of Quantity and the Signs of the Times*. Of all the titles in this short bibliography, this last mentioned is the most directly related to the Lindbom book and is without peer for eschatological doctrine.

Martin Lings. Dr. Lings is the author of a biography of the Christ-like Algerian saint, Shaikh Abu'l Abbas Ahmad ibn Mustafa 'l-'Alawi, *A Moslem Saint of the Twentieth Century*. London, 1961. This book is recommended for all who might wish to experience something of the fragrance of holiness. More directly related to the Lindbom book, however, is Lings' *Ancient Beliefs and Modern Superstitions*. London, 1965. The book focuses most strongly on Christianity, and is one of the "most powerful defenses of religion to be written in this century—if indeed 'defense' can be used of something which carries the war so persistently into the enemy camp."

Seyyed Hossein Nasr. *The Encounter of Man with Nature*, London, 1968; and his excellent and far-reaching *Knowledge and the Sacred*, New York, 1981.

Lord Northbourne. *Religion in the Modern World*, and *Looking Back on Progress*, London, 1963, and 1970, respectively. "There is nothing . . . that has nothing to do with religion, because there is nothing that has nothing to do with God."

Marco Pallis. *The Way and the Mountain*, and *A Buddhist Spectrum.*

Whitall N. Perry. *A Treasury of Traditional Wisdom*, an incomparable collection of the *philosophia perennis* from diverse sources but in its common major themes, testifying to the remarkable unanimity of the spiritual traditions of mankind.

Frithjof Schuon. All of the published works of this most perspicacious author are strongly recommended, but those listed as follows may be of especial interest in connection with the Lindbom book: *The Transcendent Unity of Religions* and *Logic and Transcendence*, both published by Harper and Row as paperback editions; and the following published by Perennial Books, London: *Light on the Ancient Worlds*, *Stations of Wisdom*, *Spiritual Perspectives and Human Facts*, and *Esoterism as Principle and as Way.*

The Sword of Gnosis, edited by Jacob Needleman, Penguin Books, U.S.A., is a collection of articles from the quarterly journal *Studies in Comparative Religion* (London). Included in the collection is Titus Burckhardt's masterly "Cosmology and Modern Science," which should be of great aid in properly situating the whole body of contemporary sciences in a context free of the exaggerated awe that too often is accorded to almost anything bearing the accolade "scientific."

MUP THE TARES AND THE GOOD GRAIN

Designed by Margaret Brown and Haywood Ellis

Composition by Omni Composition Services, Macon, Georgia
the text was 'read' by a Hendrix Typereader II OCR scanner
and was formatted by Edd Rowell on an Addressograph Multigraph Comp/Set 5404, then paginated on an A/M Comp/Set 4510.
Text type is Garamond, with headings in Friz Quadrata.

Production specifications:
text paper—60 pound Warren's Olde Style
cover (on .088 boards)—Holliston Roxite B 51538
dust jacket—100 pound enamel, printed two colors and varnished

Printing (offset lithography) by Omnipress of Macon, Inc., Macon, Georgia
Binding by John H. Dekker and Sons, Inc., Grand Rapids, Michigan